Poison Ivy and Poison Oak

This weed (above) gives you an itchy rash. Poison Ivy grows like a vine, and Poison Oak like a shrub. Try to remember what the leaves look like, and do not touch it. If you do touch it, washing your hands as soon as possible may reduce the itching. Your local drug store will also have various remedies.

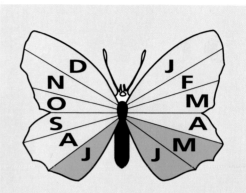

Butterfly Flight Periods

One of these symbols is shown with each species entry. It shows you at a glance the period or periods when this butterfly is in flight. This is the time of year when you are mostly like to see one.

SCIENCE NATURE GUIDES

BUTTERFLIES
OF NORTH AMERICA

Susan McKeever

ILLUSTRATIONS BY
Brian Hargreaves

CONSULTANT
Dr George C. McGavin

THUNDER BAY
P·R·E·S·S

Conservation

Over 17,300 species of butterfly live on Earth and there are more than 730 different butterflies to be found in North America. Most insects live in the tropics, and over half of them live in tropical rain forests. Many butterflies live in wetlands—like flood plains, marshes, and swamps.

Unfortunately these two habitats are the ones that are most at risk in the world today. People are felling the tropical rain forests for the hardwoods, like mahogany, to make furniture, or clearing them for farms. People are draining wetlands because they are good places to farm once the water has gone. Either way, unique butterfly species are being lost every week.

On page 78 you will find the names of some organizations who campaign for the protection of particular animals and habitats in America and around the world. By joining them and supporting their efforts, **you** can help to preserve our wildlife.

Butterfly Hunter's Code

1 **Always go collecting with a friend,** and always tell an adult where you have gone.
2 **Treat all butterflies with care**—they are delicate creatures and can be easily killed by rough handling.
3 **Ask permission** before exploring or crossing private property.
5 **Keep to footpaths** as much as possible.
6 **Keep off crops and leave fence gates** as you find them.
7 **Wear long pants, shoes, and a long-sleeved shirt** in deer tick country.
8 **Ask your parents not to light fires** except in fireplaces in special picnic areas.
9 **Take your litter home.**

Thunder Bay Press
5880 Oberlin Drive
Suite 400
San Diego, CA 92121

First published in the United States
by Thunder Bay Press, 1995

© Dragon's World, 1995
© Text Dragon's World, 1995
© Species illustrations Brian Hargreaves, 1991 & 1995
© Other illustrations Dragon's World, 1995

All rights reserved

Simplified text and captions by Susan McKeever, based on *Butterflies of North America* by John Feltwell.

Habitat paintings by Philip Weare.
Headbands by Antonia Phillips.
Identification and activities illustrations by Mr Gay Galsworthy.

Editor   Diana Briscoe
Designer   James Lawrence
Design Assistants   Karen Ferguson
                    Victoria Furbisher
Art Director   John Strange
Editorial Director Pippa Rubinstein

No part of this book may be reproduced or transmitted in any form or by any means, electronic or mechanical, including photocopy, recording, or any information storage and retrieval system, without permission in writing from Thunder Bay Press, except by a reviewer who may quote brief passages in a review.

ISBN 1–57145–018–1

Complete Cataloging in Publication (CIP) is available through the Library of Congress.
LC Card Number:

Printed in Italy

Contents

What Is a Butterfly?........**4–5**
What To Look For...................6–7

**Found Almost
Everywhere**....................**8–17**
A Butterfly Safari.................18–19

Bogs & Wetlands..........**20–29**
Butterflies To Be.................30–31

**Meadows &
Grasslands**....................**32–51**
Raising Butterflies..............42–43
Butterfly Garden.................52–53

Deserts & Mountains....**54–61**
Keeping Records.................62–63

**Woodlands
& Clearings**...................**64–77**

Find Out Some More................78
Index & Glossary.................79–81

What Is a Butterfly?

Fluttering butterflies live everywhere in North America. You can spot them in a huge variety of places—on mountains, in damp bogs, in sunny woodlands, flying through the desert, and in your own backyard. You already know that they are beautiful to look at, but they also have a fascinating lifestyle.

This book will help you to become a butterfly spotter in two ways. It only shows you the butterflies that you are most likely to see, and it puts them in the habitat, or type of countryside, where you are most likely to see them.

Where butterflies choose to live depends a lot on the flowers and plants they like to feed on. So knowing a butterfly's favorite plant, and where it grows, is a great help toward knowing where to spot that butterfly.

The life of a butterfly

Butterflies go through four very different stages in their lives, and you can look for them at each stage. The first stage is the egg. Next comes the caterpillar, the chrysalis, and finally the butterfly.

Changing from one form to another like this is called complete metamorphosis (change in form) because each stage is completely different from the last.

The caterpillar hatches (it eats its way out of the egg) and immediately starts to feed on the food plant. As it grows larger, it has to molt (shed its skin) because caterpillar skins cannot stretch.

The female butterfly lays her eggs on the plant that she knows her caterpillar likes to eat.

After shedding its skin for the last time, the caterpillar finds a twig where it can turn into a chrysalis. It spins a silken pad from which the chrysalis hangs.

How to use this book

To identify a butterfly you don't recognize, like the two shown here, follow these steps.

1 **Draw a quick sketch of the butterfly** (see page 19) in your field notebook. Draw the outline first, then fill in any other features you notice. Write down where and when you spotted the butterfly.

2 **Decide what habitat you are in.** If you read the descriptions at the start of each section, you'll soon see which one fits where you are. Each habitat has a different picture band.

3 **Look through the section with this picture band.** The picture and information given for each butterfly will help you identify it. The brightly patterned butterfly shown to the right is a Tiger Swallowtail (see page 17).

4 **If you can't find the butterfly there,** look through the other sections. Some butterflies can live in a big variety of habitats.

5 **Sometimes, the females look different to the males,** like this Cloudless Sulfur (see right and page 16). Make sure you study the pictures and the text carefully. The male (♂) and female (♀) wings are shown for each species.

6 **What month is it?** Many butterflies are seen only at certain times of the year. See the fact caption for each butterfly.

7 **If you still can't find the butterfly,** you may have to look in a larger field guide (see page 79 for some suggestions). You may have seen a very rare butterfly! Or it might be a moth (see page 53).

When the adult inside the chrysalis is fully formed, the chrysalis splits and a wet butterfly crawls out. The butterfly inflates its wings, lets them dry, and then flies off in search of nectar.

Habitat Picture Bands

This book is divided into different habitats (or types of countryside). Each habitat has a different picture band at the top of the page. These are shown below.

Found Almost Everywhere

Bogs & Wetlands

Meadows & Grasslands

Deserts & Mountains

Woodlands & Clearings

What To Look For

Parts of a butterfly

Like all insects, a typical adult butterfly has three parts to its body, and three pairs of legs. The three body parts are the head, the thorax, and the abdomen.

Each butterfly has two pairs of wings: two forewings and two hindwings. The wings are covered in scales, which give them their color. When you are trying to identify a butterfly, take note of the following:

The head has a pair of antennae, which are club-shaped at the tip, and a pair of big eyes, called compound eyes.

- Is it large or small?
- What color and shape are its wings?
- Do they have patterns on them?
- Don't forget to look under the wings, as the color and patterns there may be completely different.
- What are the antennae like?

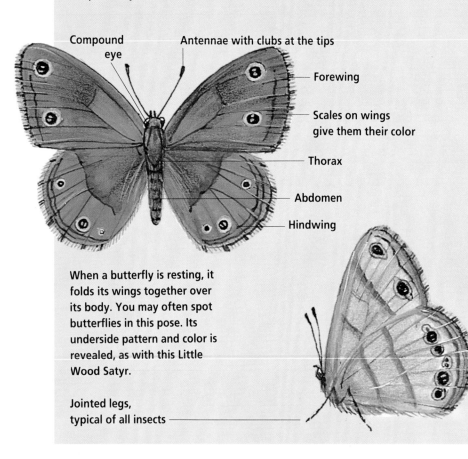

Compound eye

Antennae with clubs at the tips

Forewing

Scales on wings give them their color

Thorax

Abdomen

Hindwing

When a butterfly is resting, it folds its wings together over its body. You may often spot butterflies in this pose. Its underside pattern and color is revealed, as with this Little Wood Satyr.

Jointed legs, typical of all insects

Wing shapes

The wing shapes of butterflies vary from rounded to triangular, to long and thin. Some wings have "tails" on them; others have wavy edges.

The Gray Skipper's wings are triangular in shape

The White Admiral's hindwings have wavy edges

The Clouded Skipper's wings are pointed

The Zebra Swallowtail has a long tail on each of its hindwings

Antennae

Looking at a butterfly's antennae is a useful way to identify them as they vary from type to type.

The Swarthy Skipper, like all Skippers, has hooked antennae

The Small Parnassian's antennae are stripy

Families of Butterflies

Color & markings

The color and markings (patterns) on a butterfly's wings are one of the first things you'll notice.

The American Swallowtail has orange and black marks on its hindwings called "eyespots." These look like big eyes and frighten away would-be predators.

Male butterflies often have a black mark near the top of the forewing, like the one on this Saltgrass Skipper.

The Purple Bog Fritillary has a very noticeable pattern of black dots, dashes, and crescents against an orange background.

Swallowtails & Parnassians

These butterflies are quite large, and lively fliers. The "true" Swallowtails are all brightly colored and have tails on their hindwings.

Parnassians, like the American Apollo, are smaller and have no tails on their hindwings.

Whites & Sulfurs

Butterflies in this group are medium-sized, and are often white or yellow. Some of them have bright orange tips to their wings. Males and females often look completely different to each other, as does this Wolf-face Sulfur.

Skippers

These are the smallest of all butterflies, and also the most numerous in North America. The name "Skipper" comes from the way that they fly—with a rapid, skipping movement. Like this Greenish Little Skipper, they have very distinctive hooked antennae, and also quite hairy bodies, and triangular wings.

Brush Footed Butterflies

This is a very large family of butterflies. They are often medium-sized. The feature that really ties them together is the fact that they don't have six "working" legs, like other butterflies: their forelegs are small and are no use for walking. They are usually fast fliers.

They include the Browns, which are usually some shade of brown, the Milkweeds, and the Snouts, which have very noticeable beaklike mouth parts like this Southern Snout butterfly.

Blues, Coppers, Hairstreaks, Harvesters, & Metalmarks

These butterflies are usually small and colorful, and like wild flowers. Blues, like this Spring Azure, are usually blue; the Coppers are usually copper-colored, and the Hairstreaks usually have tails.

The Harvesters are bigger, and do not visit flowers. Metalmarks, like this Mormon Metalmark, get their name from the shiny, metallic markings on their wings that glint in the sunshine.

Found Almost Everywhere

Some butterflies feed on very common plants like nettles, and these are the ones that you are most likely to see without too much hunting. You may well see the butterflies from this section in the other habitats covered in the book—grasslands, deserts, mountains, woodlands, clearings, bogs, and wetlands. However, butterflies from those sections may also live in other types of landscape.

Roadside habitats are exactly that—grassy verges on the edges of roads. These are good places to spot butterflies, as there are often wild flowers growing there for them to visit. So next time you go for a drive, even along a highway, keep a lookout for butterflies on the grassy edges.

Parks and backyards are ideal places to spot butterflies. They are filled with colorful flowers just perfect for sipping nectar from, and leaves just waiting to be nibbled by hungry caterpillars. A more unlikely habitat is waste ground, but it often gives a home to lots of butterflies. Waste ground includes railroad yards or vacant lots and often has fast-growing weeds and hardy wild flowers growing through cracks in the concrete. The butterflies feed on very familiar weeds, such as nettles, docks, and daisies. This picture shows eight species from this section; how many can you recognize?

Spring Azure; Eastern Tailed Blue; Gray Hairstreak; Monarch; Alfalfa Orange; Tawny-tailed Skipper; Orange Dog; Swallowtail; Pipevine Swallowtail.

Found Almost Everywhere

Silver-studded Blue

Also called the Acmon Blue. Males of this butterfly have lilac-blue wings and females' wings are brown. Both males and females have a row of bright orange spots along the edge of their hindwings. They have gray undersides, also with orange spots on the hindwings. Underneath, too, there are black dots. Fringes on the edges of the wings are white. This butterfly can be seen fluttering close to the ground in pursuit of flowers in many different habitats. Its caterpillars feed on wild buckwheat, locoweed, bird's-foot trefoil, deer weed, lupine, and knotwood. It is found in Western states from Mexico to British Columbia.

Species: *Plebejus acmon* – Family: Lycaenidae
³/₄–1 ins long
Flight period: Continuous, from February to October

Small Apollo

Also known as the Small Parnassian. Males of this type of butterfly are cream colored with red spots on the hindwings, and females are darker and their wings have transparent areas. Both males and females have black and gray markings on forewings and hindwings. If you can get close enough, you will notice that they have black and white stripy antennae. The Small Apollo flies around flowery areas like meadows. Caterpillars are black with yellow spots, and feed on stonecrops. It is found from Alaska to southern California and in New Mexico.

Species:
Parnassius phoebus
Family: Papilionidae
2¹/₄–3 ins long
Flight period: One, from June to September

Cabbage Butterfly

Also known as the Small White, this butterfly is a milky white on top, and a greenish yellow underneath. You can tell the males from the females easily. Males have one black spot on each forewing, and females have two. This butterfly flies in all sorts of habitats, from backyards to fields, from cities to foothills. A very common butterfly, most gardeners will know it well. They see it as a pest, as Cabbage butterfly caterpillars, true to their name, nibble away on cabbage plants, as well as radishes and nasturtiums. The caterpillars are bright green with yellow stripes. It is found in all of the U.S. and southern Canada.

Species: *Pieris rapae* – Family: Pieridae – 1¹/₄–2 ins long
Flight period: Three to four, from March to November

Tailed Blue

So-called because of its hindwing tail, the male of this butterfly has violet-blue wings with a row of little dots on the hindwing. In the female, the wings are brown, with a single orange dot on the hindwing. Underneath, the wings are grayish white with black spots and orange spots near the tail. A white fringe runs all around the wings of males and females. Look for this butterfly fluttering close to the ground on roadsides, and in fields, backyards, and farmland areas. Caterpillars feed on clovers, beans, tick trefoil and many other types of this plant. It is found in the Eastern half of the U.S., occasionally on the West Coast.

Species: *Everes comyntas* – Family: Lycaenidae
³/₄–1 ins long
Flight period: Several flights, between spring and fall

Western Swallowtail

Also known as the Anise Swallowtail, this butterfly has thick black borders framing its wings, but it is still more yellow than black. There are yellow markings on both forewings and hindwings. Blue marks and orange eyespots appear on the hindwings. Females of this type of butterfly are bigger than the males. They fly in many areas, from forest clearings to city streets, from mountain tops to canyons. The green and black caterpillars like to munch on young leaves and buds of plants like fennel, cow parsnip, carrots, and parsley. It is found on the West Coast of North America, north to Wyoming.

Species: *Papilio zelicaon* – Family: Papilionidae
2³/₄–3 ins long
Flight period: One in the north;
all year round in the southwest

Mourning Cloak

This big butterfly is hard to miss, with its yellow border and row of blue spots against a maroon background. Underneath, the wings are dark, which is good for camouflage. You will see this butterfly in many different habitats, from forest edges to open woodlands, from backyards and parks to towns. Caterpillars, black and bristly with white speckles, feed in groups on willow, elm, hackberry, and cottonwood. It is found in most of the U.S. and Canada, except Arctic area.

Species: *Nymphalis antiopa* – Family: Nymphalidae
3–3¹/₂ ins long
Flight period: Continuous

Pipevine Swallowtail

You can recognize this butterfly by the dark gray to black forewings, and the greenish color on the hindwings. The underside of its hindwings reveals a flash of big, bright orange spots. Look out for the Pipevine Swallowtail fluttering by backyard plants like azalea, buddleia, and honeysuckle. Caterpillars of this butterfly, which are black with orange spots, eat plants that make them taste nasty, so predators like birds know to keep well away. It is found mainly in the Southeast U.S., north to the Great Lakes and may venture to the West Coast.

Species: *Battus philenor*
Family: Papilionidae
2³/₄–3¹/₂ ins long
Flight period: Two to three,
from January to October

Greenish Little Skipper

Also known as the Pepper and Salt Skipper, this butterfly has greenish brown wings, which have a brassy shine. Fringes at the edges of the wings are checkered. You can spot this butterfly resting on rocks in stony canyons and rocky slopes of mountain ranges, by roadsides, and in woodlands. It is found in Colorado and Utah, south through Southeast Arizona, New Mexico, and in West Texas.

Species: *Amblyscirtes hegon*
Family: Hesperiidae
1–1¼ ins long
Flight period: One from May to June in Colorado; from April to July in Texas; from June to September in Arizona

♂♀

Giant Swallowtail

Citrus growers see the Giant Swallowtail as quite a pest. It lays its eggs on citrus trees and its brown or olive caterpillars feed on them. The caterpillars are called Orange Dogs. Look for the Giant Swallowtail along roadsides or woodland glades, too. Very large and mostly brown, this butterfly has two broad bands of yellow spots crossing the wings, and orange spots at the base of the hindwings. Underneath, the wings are a pale yellow color. Females are much larger than the males. It is found on the East Coast from New York to Florida and west to the Mississippi River.

Species: *Papilio cresphontes*
Family: Papilionidae
3½–5½ ins long
Flight period: Continuous in the south, late spring and summer in the north

♂♀

Saltgrass Skipper

Also called the Sandhill Skipper, this butterfly is a rich brown with black and orange marks. Males, which are smaller than females, have a black mark on the forewing. Underneath, the wings are lighter, with yellow veins. The Saltgrass Skipper likes to fly around sand dunes on the coast, as well as in grassy areas, including city backyards. Caterpillars feed on grasses. It is found on the West Coast from British Columbia to Baja California.

Species: *Polites sabuleti* – Family: Hesperiidae
¾–1¼ in long – Flight period: One, from June to August

♂♀

Tawny-edged Skipper

This butterfly is so called because it has bright tawny gold patches on the edges of both forewings. This contrasts with the dark brown color of the rest of the wings. Males have a dark mark on the forewings, and females have yellow spots. Underneath, the wings are much lighter in comparison. You will find this butterfly in grassy areas, including backyards. Caterpillars, which can be either maroon or tan colored, feed on different types of grasses. It is found from coast to coast in southern Canada and northern U.S., but is rare in the Northwest.

Species: *Polites themistocles*
Family: Hesperiidae
¾–1 ins long
Flight period: One from June to August

Checkered Skipper

As its name suggests, this butterfly has a checkered pattern on its black and white wings. You can tell males from females because they have a stronger pattern. Underneath, the wings are similar in pattern, but there is an off-white band running across them. The Checkered Skipper flies in many habitats, including foothills, parks, backyards, roadsides, and riverbanks. Caterpillars feed on mallows. It is found in most of the U.S. northward into southern Canada.

Species: *Pyrgus communis* – Family: Hesperiidae
³/₄–1¹/₄ ins long
Flight period: Numerous, all year round in Texas

American Swallowtail

Also known as the Black Swallowtail, this butterfly has a row of yellow spots and a yellow band across its black wings, and an orange-red eyespot on each hindwing. There is also a scattering of blue across the hindwings, and this is stronger in the females of the species. The undersides of the wings also have spots, which may be yellow or orange. These butterflies like to fly around open spaces, like backyards, meadows, and farmland. Parsley or carrot plants will attract them to your backyard. The caterpillars, colored white or green with black bands, feed on Queen Anne's lace, carrot plants, and citrus plants. It is found from Manitoba to Maine, south to Florida, and west to southern California.

Species: *Papilio polyxenes*
Family: Papilionidae
2³/₄–3¹/₂ ins long
Flight period: Three, from February to November

Common Sooty Wing

Also known as the Roadside Rambler, this little butterfly has long, rounded wings, which are black or dark brown. There are crescent-shaped white spots running down each forewing, and sometimes on the hindwing. You will find this butterfly in many habitats, from waste ground and weedy areas in cities to low mountains. Its caterpillars, which are pale green with a dark head, feed on pigweed, cheeseweed, and lamb's quarters. It is found in most of the U.S., especially California and Baja California.

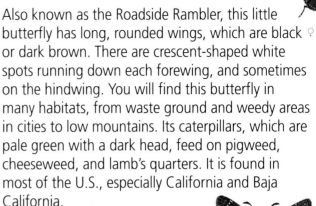

Species: *Pholisora catullus*
Family: Hesperiidae
1–1¹/₄ ins long
Flight period: Two, from May to September

Gray Skipper

The Gray Skipper is quite a plain butterfly, with little pattern. It has triangular wings which are a gray-brown color. There are some small white spots on the forewings. Underneath, the forewing is tan, and the hindwing is brown with gray "dusting." You'll find this butterfly in many habitats, from pine woods to desert valleys, from coasts to roadsides. The caterpillars are bright green with yellow patches and feed on grasses. It is found in most of the southern U.S., north to Nebraska, east to Virginia, and south to Argentina.

Species: *Lerodea eufala*
Family: Hesperiidae
1–1¹/₄ ins long
Flight period: One during early spring in the north; two in Georgia from March to April and from August to September

Found Almost Everywhere

Mormon Metalmark

Brightly patterned with white spots and black markings against shades of brown and orange, this butterfly should be easy to spot. It flies swiftly and basks in the sunshine in many habitats, from beaches to mountains and deserts. It is very common all over the West Coast. Dark gray caterpillars feed on different kinds of buckwheats. It is found on the entire West Coast of the U.S. north to Montana.

Species: *Apodemia mormo*
Family: Riodinidae
³/₄–1¹/₄ ins long
Flight period: One to two, from March to October

Brown Elfin

This very common butterfly has warm brown wings, with an orange tinge in the females. Males have a black mark on their forewings. Underneath, the wings are light brown. The Brown Elfin flies in woodland glades, chaparral, deserts, and shrubby forests. Its caterpillars feed on many plants, including blueberries, bearberry, azalea, dodder, lilac, and apples. It is widespread from Alaska to Newfoundland, south to Georgia and Baja California.

Species: *Callophrys augustus*
Family: Lycaenidae
³/₄–1¹/₄ ins long
Flight period: One, from February to June

Gray Hairstreak

Also known as the Common Hairstreak. The wings of this butterfly are a rich gray-brown with orange spots on the bottom of the hindwings. Each hindwing has two tails, one long, one short. Underneath, the wings are light gray with an orange and white line across them, and orange patches on the hindwings. This butterfly can be found in many places, from woodlands to coastlines, from parks to roadsides. The green caterpillars have many favored foods, including corn, oak, cotton, strawberry, and mint. It is found everywhere in the U.S. and across southern Canada.

Species: *Strymon melinus*
Family: Lycaenidae
1–1¹/₄ ins long
Flight period: Two to three in the south, from April to October

Banded Hairstreak

It is easy to tell the males from the females of this butterfly as males have a large oval mark on their forewings. Both males and females have brownish black wings, and hindwings have two tails each, one long and one short. Underneath the wings are crossed by two rows of lines, and there are orange marks at the base of the hindwings. The Banded Hairstreak sips nectar from milkweed, dogbane, daisies, and sumac. They live in waysides, forests, parks, and backyards. Yellow-green or brownish caterpillars feed on walnuts, hickories, and oaks. It is found in Southern Canada and the eastern half of the U.S. except the tip of Florida.

Species: *Satyrium calanus*
Family: Lycaenidae
1–1¹/₄ ins long
Flight period: One from June to July

Painted Lady

Orange, black, white, and brown marks cover the Painted Lady's wings and the tips of the forewings are mainly black with white spots. A look underneath the hindwings reveals four blue spots on an olive-green background. This butterfly is not fussy about its habitat, it flies just about anywhere, especially flowery areas. Caterpillars, purplish and spiny, like to eat thistles. It is found in most of the U.S., northward into Canada as far as the Arctic Circle.

Species: *Vanessa cardui* – Family: Nymphalidae
About 2 ins long
Flight period: Continuous in the south

♂♀   ♂

Spring Azure

This butterfly has sky blue wings, with brown borders in the female. Underneath, the wings are slate gray with a black checkered border and black spots on the hindwings. As its name suggests, this butterfly is very common in the early spring, and if you see it, you will know that spring has arrived. The Spring Azure flies in many types of habitat, from woodlands and roadsides, to mountains, clearings, and glades. Caterpillars feed on many types of flowers, including dogwoods, viburnum, and meadowsweets. It is found right across the U.S. and into Canada as far as Alaska and northern Quebec.

♂♀

♂

Species:
Celastrina argiolus
Family: Lycaenidae
3/4–1 1/4 ins long
Flight period:
Between one
and several

Red Admiral

This butterfly has bright red bars crossing its forewings. The top of the forewings are black and spotted with white. The hindwings have orange bars on their borders. Underneath, the wings have a mottled pattern with black, brown, and blue. The Red Admiral flies in all sorts of areas, from flowery meadows to rivers and shorelines, from forest clearings to cities. Caterpillars, spiny and patterned with brown, black, and tan, feed on nettles. It is found in most of the U.S. and northward to Hudson Bay and Alaska.

Species: *Vanessa atalanta* – Family: Nymphalidae
1 3/4–2 1/4 ins long
Flight period: Continuous in the south

♂♀

♂

Found Almost Everywhere

Cloudless Sulfur

Males of this type of butterfly are always bright yellow, but females are often pale cream with a dark margin, so can look completely different. Underneath, the wings are lemon-yellow with reddish brown marks. Look for this butterfly flying around open spaces like backyards, glades, meadows, and coasts. Its caterpillars are yellow or greenish, and feed on partridge pea, sennas, and clovers. It is found in Mexico and Florida, and north to the Great Lakes.

Species: *Phoebis sennae*
Family: Pieridae – 2¼–2¾ ins long
Flight period: Continuous in the south, two toward the north

Alfalfa Butterfly

Also known as the Orange Sulfur, you would find it hard to miss this bright orange butterfly. The females are a paler orange than the males, and have yellow spots on the black border of their wings. Males just have a solid black border. Look for the black spot on the forewings of both males and females. Underneath, the hindwing is lemon-yellow. The wings have a pink fringe around them. The Alfalfa Sulfur likes to fly just about anywhere, especially around alfalfa fields. Its caterpillars are dark green with pink and white stripes and white hair. They feed on alfalfa and white clover. It is found in most of the U.S., except West Coast and southeast, and in Canada from Alaska to Ontario.

Species: *Colias eurytheme*
Family: Pieridae
1¾–2½ ins long
Flight period: Continuous from March to December

Bronze Copper

This is a big butterfly with different colored males and females. Males are dark copper-brown with a purple sheen on their forewings, while hindwings are shiny gray with an orange margin. Females are bright orange with dark spots and a brown margin on the forewings, while their hindwings are dark gray with dark spots and an orange margin. Easy to spot because of its size and bright color, the Bronze Copper can be seen in damp meadows, swamps, and ditches. Caterpillars, which are bright yellowish green, feed on docks like curly dock, and also on knotweeds, which grow in moist areas. It is found from the Northwest Territories to Maine and south to Wyoming and Arkansas.

Species: *Lycaena hyllus*
Family: Lycaenidae
1¼–1½ ins long
Flight period: Two from June to July and from August to October

Whirlabout

Males and females of this butterfly look completely different. The males have yellow-orange wings and the females wings are dull brown with a few light marks on the forewings. The name "Whirlabout" comes from this butterfly's way of flying in rapid circles. Look in grassy habitats like scrub and rolling hills for the Whirlabout, as well as grassy sites in cities. Caterpillars feed on hairy paspalum and weedy lawn grasses. It is found in Arkansas and Virginia south to Texas and west to Arizona, as far south as Argentina.

Species: *Polites vibex*
Family: Hesperiidae
1–1¼ ins long
Flight period: Continuous in the south; fewer in the north

Spicebush Swallowtail

Look for a butterfly that is mostly brown on the forewings, and greenish blue on the hindwings. This is the Spicebush Swallowtail. Creamy yellow spots frame the wings. There are two bright orange spots on each hindwing, one at the top and one at the bottom. Underneath the wings, there are two rows of orange-red spots. You will find this butterfly in backyards, woods, meadows, fields, and forests. The dark green caterpillars eat spicebush, sassafras, and bays. It is found east of the Mississippi.

Species: *Pterourus troilus* – Family: Papilionidae
3½–4½ in long – Flight period: From April to October

Tiger Swallowtail

It is easy to see how this butterfly got its name, from its black tiger stripes against a yellow background. The hindwings often have a row of blue patches, with orange spots. A darker form of the Tiger Swallowtail exists, in which the females are black with yellow spots. This is a butterfly that you are very likely to see, as it lives throughout North America. Look out for Tiger Swallowtails feeding in groups from flowers. Their caterpillars start off brown and white, and then turn green. They feed on broad-leaved trees and shrubs, like willows, birches, and ashes. It is found in most of North America and Alaska, except within the Arctic Circle.

Species:
Pterourus
glaucus
Family:
Papilionidae
3¼–5½ ins long
Flight period:
One, from
March to
November

Monarch

This is a butterfly which is hard to miss, because of its great size, and also because of its bright orange color and stylish black patterns. It has black veins crossing its wings, and a black border sprinkled with white spots. You've probably seen it, as it is one of the most common butterflies of all, and can be seen all over the U.S. The Monarch flutters around flowery waysides. The caterpillars of the Monarch, which are off-white with black and yellow stripes, feed on milkweeds, which make them poisonous if eaten. Many a hungry predator has to learn this lesson the hard way! It is found everywhere in the U.S.

Species:
Danaus
plexippus
Family:
Danaidae
3½–4 ins long
Flight period:
Several as it migrates both north and south every year

A Butterfly Safari

Wherever you go butterfly-watching, there are a few items which will be valuable to you. The main things that you need are this guide book and your field notebook.

Essential equipment

When you go looking for insects, it is a good idea to take these pieces of equipment with you:

1 **Hand lens:** helps you to look at a basking butterfly or a caterpillar on a leaf close up and in great detail. Buy a folding one that magnifies things 4 or 6 times (labeled x4 or x6) and wear it on a cord around your neck.

2 **Glass or plastic jars** with holes bored in the lid: useful if you find a large caterpillar and want to put it somewhere safe while you look at it.

3 **A little paintbrush:** useful if you want to lift up a caterpillar for a closer look.

4 **Aerial net:** for trapping butterflies and moths temporarily (see opposite.)

5 **Beating tray, sheet, or pale umbrella:** for investigating trees and bushes (see page 31.)

6 **Camera:** you can take a quick snapshot of what you see and the habitat in which you have found it.

7 **Binoculars:** useful if you want to watch butterflies at a distance or in flight.

8 **Pair of gloves:** some caterpillars can give you a nasty rash from their prickly hairs.

9 **Field notebook and pens:** always take notes of the weather, the date, where you go, and what you find.

10 **Box of colored pencils:** for field sketches of butterflies.

11 **Lightweight backpack:** this is the most comfortable way to carry your equipment and leaves your hands free.

Field sketches

When you see a butterfly you don't recognize, make a quick sketch in your field notebook. If you start looking it up in your guide book, it will have flown away by the time you find it! Draw its outline first, then fill in more important details, using your colored pencils. Points to look for are:

- What size was the butterfly? Record a quick estimation of its wingspan.
- Was it one plain color? Note it down.
- Was the butterfly patterned? What colors and shapes were the different patterns?
- Could you see what its antennae were like?
- What kind of flower was it feeding from?
- Did it fly in a particular way (see page 7)?

Also, make a note of the habitat you were in when you spotted the butterfly. This will make it easier for you to look it up in your field guide later.

Turn the mouth of the net downward to stop the butterfly escaping.

Press the net gently against the ring to trap the butterfly at the bottom.

Using an aerial net

It is best to buy a lightweight aerial net from a company that specializes in supplying insect-collecting equipment. The net itself should be made of 28 gauge nylon or muslin. The trick is to turn the mouth of the net sideways, once the butterfly is inside. Then the mouth of the net will be covered by material and the butterfly cannot escape.

Hold a butterfly only by its folded wings, very gently between your thumb and forefinger.

Bogs & Wetlands

These damp, watery areas include pond and river banks, marshes, swamps, and peat bogs. The water can be fresh or salt. Bogs have very acidic soil where only certain plants, such as cranberries and lichens, can grow. Many bogs occur in the far North of the United States. You may also find boggy areas in the middle of forests and on mountainsides.

Around wetland areas, you may see large groups of butterflies gathered around muddy puddles, drinking the water. This is called mud-puddling, and provides the butterflies with special minerals. It is a common sight in warmer climates, and is an ideal moment to observe them.

Butterflies that live in bog and wetland habitats are particularly at risk from pollution from houses, cars, and factories. The places that they live are also at risk from the damage that is caused to them when nearby lands are drained for farming.

When looking around wetlands for butterflies, tread very carefully—you may sink into the mushy ground. This picture shows nine species from this section; how many can you recognize?

Red-disk Alpine; Forest Arctic; Cinquefoil Copper; Forest Copper; Hoary Elfin; Atlantis Fritillary; Purple Bog Fritillary; Swamp Metalmark; Yellow Parnassian.

Bogs & Wetlands

White-spot Alpine

Also known as the Spruce Bog Alpine because it likes moist bogs, this butterfly has wings that are brownish or black, with four eyespots with orange rims on each forewing. Underneath the forewings, there is the same eyespot pattern. A look under the hindwings will show how the butterfly got its name, as there are two white spots here. You may see this butterfly drinking from mud puddles. Its caterpillars may feed on meadow grass. It is found from Alaska to Newfoundland.

Species: *Erebia disa*
Family: Satyridae
3/4–2 ins long
Flight period: One, from June to July

Forest Arctic

Also called the Jutta Arctic, this dark gray or brown butterfly has a pale orange band running down both sets of wings. Inside the orange color, there are black spots. Underneath the hindwing, you will see a mottled grayish pattern that looks a bit like tree bark. This butterfly likes bogland and forests. The caterpillar has olive stripes, and feeds on cotton grass. It is found from Alaska to Newfoundland, south to Wyoming.

Species: *Oeneis jutta*
Family: Satyridae
2–2¼ ins long
Flight period: One, from May to August

Red-disk Alpine

Look for the red color on the forewings of this butterfly that gives it its name. The rest of the wings are blackish brown, with no eyespots visible anywhere. Underneath, the wings are mottled brown and gray. Its caterpillars feed on meadow grasses and sedges growing in the meadows and prairies in which it lives. It is found from Alaska to Quebec.

Species: *Erebia discoidalis*
Family: Satyridae
1¾–2 ins long
Flight period: One, from May to July

Western Skipperling

♂♀   ♀

Also called the Garita Skipperling, this small butterfly has brownish wings with a gold dusting on them that glints in the light. The edges of the forewings are reddish. Underneath, the hindwings are gray with pale orange, and the forewings are orange at the tip. You will find this butterfly flying around meadows and grassland, especially where the ground is moist. Caterpillars, green with white lines, feed on different types of grasses. It is found in Southern Canada west of the Great Lakes, and south to Mexico.

Species: *Oarisma garita* – **Family: Hesperiidae**
3/4–1 ins long
Flight period: One, from June to August

Aspen Dusky Wing

Also called the Dreamy Dusky Wing, this butterfly's wings are rounded and are a gray-brown color. There are gray spots on the forewings, and two rows of pale spots on the hindwings. Underneath, the wings look similar. This butterfly can be found in forest clearings and wet meadows. It lays its eggs on a variety of trees. The caterpillars are light green with white speckles, and feed on willow, poplars, locusts, and birches. It is found as far north as the Northwest Territories in Canada and south to Georgia, westward to Arizona.

Species: *Erynnis icelus*
Family: Hesperiidae
1–1½ ins long
Flight period: One, from May to June

♂♀   ♂

Southern Pearly Eye

This butterfly is brownish tan, with eyespots running down its wings. Look at the arrangement of the forewing eyespots, which run in a crooked line. Called the Southern Pearly Eye because it lives mostly in the southeastern U.S., you will see this butterfly on tree trunks in woodlands, and also by streams and in backyards. Caterpillars are yellow-green with red-tipped horns, and feed on cane, a type of grass. It is found in the Southeast U.S., except most of Florida.

Species:
Lethe portlandia
Family: Satyridae
1¾–2 ins long
Flight period: Continuous, from April to November

♂♀

Marsh Eyed Brown

A warm tan color on top, with rounded wings, the Marsh Eyed Brown has dark spots near the margins of both wings. A look underneath the wings shows a light velvety brown color with darker, zigzag lines, as well as a row of eyespots with yellow rims. This butterfly likes a damp habitat, such as open, damp, meadows, sedge marshes, and wet parts of prairies. Caterpillars, light green with yellow and dark green stripes, feed on sedges. It is found in the Northwest Territories to Quebec, and south to central U.S.

Species: *Lethe eurydice*
Family: Satyridae
1¾–2 ins long
Flight period: Two, from June to August

♂♀

Greenish Clover Blue

This name comes from the males' wing color, which is silvery blue with a greenish tinge. Females have two forms, either brown or blue. Underneath, both males and females are paler with dark spots. The Greenish Blue flies in damp, clover meadows in the summer, and also by roadsides, streamsides and in bogs. Caterpillars, which are greenish or reddish, feed on clover flowers. It is found from Alaska to Maine and northwestern U.S.

Species: *Plebejus saepiolus*
Family: Lycaenidae
1–1¼ ins long
Flight period: One or two, from June to July

Hoary Elfin

This little butterfly has dark brown wings with white and black edging. Underneath, there is a silvery gray frosting on the edges of the wings, hence the name "hoary," from hoar frost. This butterfly is a signal that spring has arrived, for it is then that they first appear. They fly in rocky areas, scrub, and heathland. Young caterpillars feed on bearberry flowers, where they are well camouflaged by their rosy color. It is found from Alaska to Baja California and to Newfoundland and south to Georgia and Alabama.

Species: *Callophrys polios* – Family: Lycaenidae
¾–1 ins long
Flight period: One, from March to June

Two-spot Sedge Skipper

This butterfly has dark brown pointed wings. Females have two tiny yellowish spots on their forewings. Underneath the forewings, both males and females have two bright yellow spots against a dark orange background. Under the hindwings, you will see a dark tan color with bright yellow veins. Look for this butterfly around bogs, marshes, and sedge meadows. The caterpillars feed on sedges. It is found from Ontario to Nebraska, Colorado to Maine, and south along the coast to the Carolinas.

Species: *Euphyes bimacula*
Family: Hesperiidae
About 1¼ ins long
Flight period: One, from late June to July

Baltimore

This butterfly's dark wings have clear orange marks on the outside margins, next to rows of pale yellow spots. Underneath, the wings look similar, but they have more white and orange color. The females are more patterned and bigger than the males. Named in the 1600s for the first Lord Baltimore whose coat of arms was the same color, this butterfly lives around meadows and bogs. The caterpillars are black with orange strips and black spines, and feed on turtlehead, false foxglove, plantain, and white ash. It is found east of the Mississippi River.

Species:
Euphydryas phaeton
Family: Nymphalidae
1¾–2½ ins long
Flight period: One, from May to June

Pale Tiger Swallowtail

The pale cream background color on the wings give this butterfly its name. Thick black stripes cross the wings, with broad black borders spotted with cream. At the bottom of the hindwings are blue and orange markings, above and below. Look out for the Pale Tiger flying in patterns around buckthorn bushes. It likes hilltops, where it drinks nectar from mints and thistles. Caterpillars, colored green, yellow, and black, feed on mountain plants, including mountain lilac, holly-leaf cherry, and coffeeberry. It is found from British Columbia to southern California and New Mexico.

♀

Species: *Pterourus eurymedon*
Family: Papilionidae
3–3¾ ins long
Flight period: One, from April to July

Swamp Metalmark

This little butterfly has quite pointed brown wings, with fine black spots and dashes. Underneath the wings have completely different bright orange marking with black patterns. As its name suggests, the Swamp Metalmark likes wet areas such as swamps. It has pale green caterpillars which feed on swamp thistle. It is found east and south of the Great Lakes to Arkansas.

♂♀

♂

Species: *Calephelis muticum*
Family: Lycaenidae
1–1¼ ins long
Flight period: One to two, from July to September

Northern Willow Hairstreak

Also called the Acadian Hairstreak, this butterfly is easy to identify, with its dark brown color and one orange spot on each hindwing near the tail. Underneath, the wings are silvery gray, and the male has a blue spot near the tail. This butterfly likes to fly around damp fields and meadows, especially where there are willows growing, because their green and yellow caterpillars munch on willows. It is found across the U.S. from Washington State to Maine and in southern Canada.

♂♀

Species: *Satyrium acadica*
Family: Lycaenidae
About 1¼ ins long
Flight period:
One, from June to July

Forest Copper

This butterfly's other name is the Mariposa Copper, from "mariposa," the Spanish word for butterfly. Males of this butterfly look a little different from the females. They have copper-brown wings with a purple tinge and a dark border. Females can be recognized by their bright orange spots, mostly on the forewings. Underneath, the hindwings are gray with black patterns, while the forewing undersides are copper with a gray margin. You can spot this butterfly in bogs and wet meadows. It is found from the Yukon in Canada to California, eastward to Wyoming.

Species: *Lycaena mariposa*
Family: Lycaenidae – 1–1¼ ins long
Flight period: One, from July to August

Zigzag Fritillary

Also known as Willow-bog Fritillary and Freya's Fritillary, the name "Freya" coming from the Norse goddess of love and beauty. This butterfly is dark orange with a black pattern of spots and bands, and can be easily identified by looking underneath its hindwing. Here, you will see large dashes, with white bars near the margin, and a zigzag red and white band in the middle. It flies in forest clearings and willow bogs, and also around Arctic tundra. Caterpillars are brown and spiny with creamy spots, and feed on dwarf and alpine blueberry that grow around its habitat. It is found from Alaska to Newfoundland.

Species: *Boloria freija*
Family: Nymphalidae
1¼–1½ ins long
Flight period: One, from May to July

Cranberry Bog Copper

Can you guess how this butterfly got its name? It is because its caterpillars like to eat cranberries and blueberries, which grow in bogland. Sometimes it is simply called the "Bog Copper." The male of this little butterfly has brown wings with a purple sheen, while the female is grayish with black specks. Underneath, both males and females are much lighter colored, yellow or white, also with black specks. Look near cranberry bushes in bogs and you will see these butterflies flying around, or perching on the berries. It is found from Indiana to Newfoundland.

Species: *Lycaena epixanthe*
Family: Lycaenidae
About 1 ins long
Flight period: One, from June to August

Cinquefoil Copper

Also known as the Dorcas Copper. Males of this butterfly are easy to spot, as they have a very bright purple sheen on their wings, which have a wide brown margin. The females have no purple on their wings; instead they have orange and black spots on a dark brown background. Underneath, both males and females are dull yellowish brown. They like to fly around meadows and clearings, as well as bogs, where they visit flowers. Caterpillars feed on cinquefoils, which is where the name comes from. It is found in the Northwest Territories eastward to Newfoundland, south to Ohio.

Species: *Lycaena dorcas*
Family: Lycaenidae
1–1¼ ins long
Flight period: One, from July to August

Broad-winged Skipper

Also called the Broad Marsh Skipper, and true to its name, this butterfly has full, broad wings. The male's wings are dark brown with orange spots on the forewings, and a broad margin on the hindwings. Females look similar except that some have white spots on their forewings. Underneath, hindwings are a rusty tan color. This butterfly lives around marshland, and has gray-brown caterpillars that feed on marsh millet, wild rice, and lake sedge. It is found in Minnesota east to Maine, south to Alabama, west to Texas, and north to Nebraska.

Species:
Poanes viator
Family:
Hesperiidae
1¼–1¾ ins long
Flight period:
Varies, from April to August

♂♀

Golden Sulfur

♀   ♂♀

Also known as the Western Sulfur. Male Golden Sulfurs are lemon yellow with dark margins, females are a paler yellow color, with gray markings on the wings, pink fringes, and pink legs. Underneath the wings, both males and females are a dark orange-yellow. Look for this butterfly flying by the sea, in meadows and clearings, open pine and Douglas fir forest, and on mountain slopes. Caterpillars eat vetch and white sweet clover. It is found from British Columbia to California.

Species: *Colias occidentalis*
Family: Pieridae
1½–2 ins long
Flight period: One, from June to August

American Apollo

Also known as the Clodius Parnassian, this is a butterfly with big rounded wings. In the male, the wings are cream with a black and red spot. The female has big gray patches. Both males and females have red spots on the hindwings. The American Parnassian likes to fly around coasts, shaded canyons, and open mountain woods. You may see it flying along, slowly and deliberately, feeding on nectar from different wild flowers. Caterpillars, usually black with yellow or red spots, feed on the Bleeding Heart plant. It is found in Southern California and Utah to Alaska.

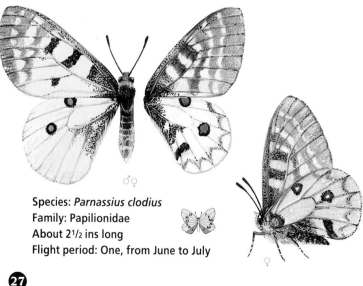

♂♀

Species: *Parnassius clodius*
Family: Papilionidae
About 2½ ins long
Flight period: One, from June to July

♀

Bogs & Wetlands

Regal Fritillary

A very large butterfly, the Regal Fritillary has orange forewings with black marks, and black hindwings with two rows of creamy colored spots. A look underneath the hindwings will reveal a deep brown color with lots of pale yellow spots. This butterfly likes to fly around wet meadows and grasslands. Sadly, a lot of the grassland is now being plowed and developed, so its habitat is disappearing. Caterpillars, yellow, brown, and black with spines, feed on violets. It is found from the central U.S. to the East Coast.

Species: *Speyeria idalia* – **Family: Nymphalidae**
2³/₄–3³/₄ ins long
Flight period: One, from June to September

Atlantis Fritillary

You can tell the male from the female Atlantis Fritillaries by the color. Males are deep orange, and females are much paler. Both sexes have black bars, spots, and crescent shapes on their wings, a pattern that continues underneath the forewings. There are silver spots under the hindwing. You will find this butterfly around flowery open spaces, including woodlands, along streams, or in wet meadows. It is to be seen in different guises in many parts of the U.S. Caterpillars are purplish with orange spines, and feed on many types of violets. It is found from Alaska to Newfoundland and south to Arizona.

Species: *Speyeria atlantis*
Family: Nymphalidae
1³/₄–2³/₄ ins long
Flight period: One, from July to August

Viceroy

Easy to notice with its rich orange color and black lattice pattern of veins, the Viceroy also has white-spotted black borders on its wings, and white spots run diagonally across the top of each forewing. This butterfly likes to fly by rivers, marshes, and meadows, as well as roadsides and waysides. It has mottled brown or olive caterpillars, which like to feed on willows, but will also try poplars, apples, cherries, and plums. It is found in the Northwest Territories to Newfoundland, south to Florida, some in the southwestern U.S. south into Mexico.

Species: *Basilarchia archippus*
Family: Nymphalidae – 2³/₄–3 ins long
Flight period: Three, from May to September

Ocellate Fritillary

Look for this small butterfly in the bogs and marshes that give it its other name, the Bog Fritillary. It is orange with dark spots, and the pattern continues under the forewing. Under the hindwing, you can see cream or silver bands, and a row of black-rimmed pearly spots. This butterfly lays its eggs, and hides among mosses waiting for the sun to come out and warm it up. Caterpillars, reddish brown and spiny, feed on a variety of willow and violet plants, freely available in boglands. It is found from Alaska to Newfoundland.

Species: *Boloria eunomia*
Family: Nymphalidae
1¼–1½ ins long
Flying period: One, from June to August

Purple Bog Fritillary

Also called Titania's Fritillary, this butterfly is dark orange with a very strong black pattern of dots, dashes, and crescents. The underside of the hindwing is a dark, often purplish color, with white marks, and a ring of white spots. You can see this butterfly around bogs, tundra, mountainsides, roadside, and alpine meadows. Caterpillars feed on willows, bistort, and violets. It is found on the Greenland coast and south from Canada to New Mexico.

Species: *Boloria titania*
Family: Nymphalidae
1¼–1¾ ins long
Flight period: One, from June to August

American Painted Lady

This brightly patterned butterfly has orange, pink, black, white, and blue marks on its wings, and a border of white and black. The best way to identify it is to look underneath the hindwings. Here, you will find two large eyespots against an olive-green background. This butterfly is fond of flowery, open, sunny spots, such as backyards, and streams. Caterpillars, black with yellow stripes and white spots, feed on evergreens. It is found throughout most of the U.S.

Species: *Vanessa virginiensis*
Family: Nymphalidae
1¾–2¼ ins long
Flight period: Three, from March to October

Green Comma

Also called the Faunus Anglewing. This butterfly is a dark orange color with black blotches and yellow spots running alongside a dark margin. The outline of the wings is very uneven and ragged. Why is it called the Green Comma? A look underneath the wings will show you. Here, there are two rows of green bars on a brown background, as well as a silver comma shape. This butterfly likes the banks of streams, coniferous woodlands, and glades, where it sunbathes and feeds. Caterpillars, tan with white patches and spines, feed on birch, alder, willow, and currant. It is found from Alaska to Newfoundland, south to California and Georgia.

Species: *Polygonia faunus*
Family: Nymphalidae
About 2 ins long
Flight period: One, from June to October

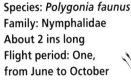

Butterflies To Be

Most butterflies spend far more time as a caterpillar and a chrysalis than they do as a butterfly (see page 4). If you can find them at an earlier stage, you can watch them develop into an adult butterfly.

Beating for caterpillars

A good way to see tree- or shrub-dwelling caterpillars more clearly is to dislodge them from the branches. You can do this with a sharp blow from a long stick on the branch. Try beating several different types of trees—some caterpillars will feed only on one type.

1 **Stretch a white sheet out under a low tree branch** or make a beating tray (see opposite for how to do it). You can also use a pale umbrella turned upside-down.
2 **Find a long stick** and beat the base of the branch quite sharply. Take care not to damage the tree.
3 **Many different insects, including caterpillars, should drop** onto the beating tray.
4 **You may find it easier** if one person holds the beating tray, and the other uses the stick.

Collecting pupae

Looking for paupae(chrysalises) while out on a country walk can be a challenging task. Some may be buried in the ground or in a pile of leaves. Others may be impossible to spot, as they are so well camouflaged (hidden against the background).

Just like caterpillars, chrysalises need to be inconspicuous. Some chrysalises look like leaves or twigs. Some even have ragged edges and holes that add to the effect. Tiny silver or gold spots on a chrysalis mimic drops of rain. Sometimes they imitate bird droppings, which would be sure to keep any predator (hunter) at bay! Other types of chrysalises seem to draw attention to themselves with bright colors. This shows they are poisonous, so a predator would risk its life.

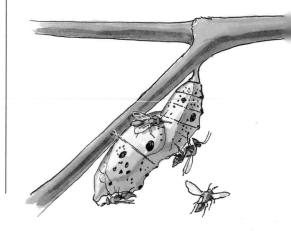

1 **When you have found your chrysalis,** make notes about where you found it. You can also make a color drawing, noting the way in which it was camouflaged. What was it imitating—a leaf perhaps, or a bird dropping?

2 **Carefully place the pupa in a glass or plastic jar** (see page 18.)

3 **Take off the lid at home.** Cover the jar with cheesecloth or screening, and put it in the shade.

4 **Check your pupa regularly**—every two days or so in the spring.

5 **When it hatches,** take note of what emerges. You may discover that small wasps crawl out. Many types of insects lay their eggs inside the eggs or caterpillars of butterflies: they are known as parasites.

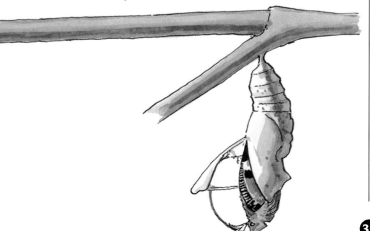

Make a beating tray

An easy way to look at caterpillars that live on trees is to make a beating tray. You will need: two bamboo canes about 30 inches long, one bamboo cane 3 feet long, some white cloth (a piece of old bedsheet will do), strong glue or a stapler, some string or wire, and a long stick.

1 **Place one of the short canes across the top of the long cane** to make a "T" shape and secure it tightly with some string or wire.

2 **Then lay the other short cane across the middle of the long cane** and fix it with wire or string so that it cannot move around.

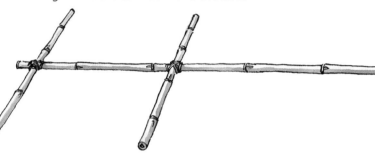

3 **Cut enough white cloth to lay across the bamboo frame** and overlap the edges by 2 inches all around.

4 **Lay the cloth on the ground, then lay the frame on top.** Fold the edges of the cloth over the frame and fix it with fabric glue or staples. If this is difficult, ask an adult to help you. If you glue it, don't use the tray until the glue is dry.

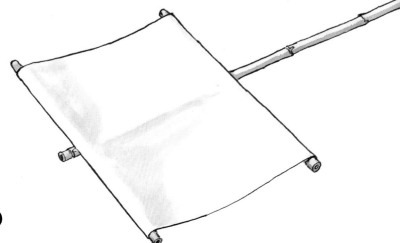

Meadows & Grasslands

Wide, flat, open spaces filled with different types of grasses or flowers are typical of these habitats. They are exposed to wind, rain, and sunshine, and get little shelter. Meadows, fields, and pastures are often teeming with wild flowers such as sheep sorrel and clovers, to which butterflies such as the Small Copper and the Golden Sulfur are attracted.

American grasslands are known as prairies and occur in a broad belt down the middle of the country. Within this belt, there are three main types of prairie. Towards the East, the prairie is moist and has tall grasses. It runs from Ohio down to eastern Oklahoma. Towards the West, in the shadow of the Rockies, the grasslands are dry. In between the two, the prairies have medium-height grasses.

Many butterflies that live in prairies lay their eggs on various grasses, so that their caterpillars can eat them when they hatch. Sadly, much of the American prairie is being destroyed by over-grazing by farm animals, and plowing the land to grow cultivated grasses. This means that a butterfly's favorite plant disappears, leaving it at a loss. This picture shows fourteen species from this section; how many can you recognize?

Zebra Swallowtail.
European Skipperling; Least Skipperling; Pink-edged Sulfur;
Blazing Star Skipper; Prairie Skipper; Swarthy Skipper;
Western Orangetip; Grasshopper Satyr;
Silver Meadow Fritillary; Large Wood Nymph;
Mottled Arctic; Greenish Blue; Purplish Copper;

Lupine Blue

Also known as the Common Blue, males of this butterfly are silver blue with dark margins. Females are mostly brown, with some blue at the bases of their wings. Underneath, both males and females are pale gray or cream with black spots. This butterfly is fond of any areas where lupine grows, such as mountains, valleys, meadows, and roadsides. The lupine is the plant that its caterpillars feed on. It is found from the western U.S. north into Canada.

Species: *Plebejus icarioides*
Family: Lycaenidae
1–1½ ins long
Flight period: One,
from April to August

White-M Hairstreak

This is a striking butterfly, with its iridescent bright blue forewings enclosed by a dark margin. Look underneath the wings and you will see the reason for the name. There is a clear "M" shape near the base of each hindwing, in white and black. In this area, too, there are orange, black, and blue spots. Each forewing has two tails, one short, and one long. Look for the White-M Hairstreak flying rapidly around grassy meadows and clearings in woods, often near oaks. Caterpillars, which are a light yellow-green color, feed on oak trees. It is found from New York to Texas, including southern states, and Florida.

Species: *Parrhasius m-album*
Family: Lycaenidae
1¼–1½ ins long
Flight period:
Three in the south;
two in the North, from
February to August

Orange-margined Blue

The female Orange-margined Blue has the brown and bluish gray wings with orange margins that give this butterfly its name. Males look different, with wings of vivid blue with narrow black margins. Underneath, the wings are pale with an orange band. Look in alfalfa fields for this butterfly, as it is here that their caterpillars munch alfalfa flowers and leaves. They also eat lupine. They are also found in clearings in shrubland and prairie. It is found in the western U.S., northeast to Maine, north into Canada.

Species: *Plebejus melissa* – **Family: Lycaenidae**
1–1¼ ins long
Flight period: Two, from May to August

Long-tailed Skipper

The large Long-tailed Skipper lives up to its name with its half-inch-long hindwing tail. The wings are dark brown with a band of white spots across the forewings, and a bright blue-green sheen on the forewing base, hindwings, and body. Underneath, the wings are duller, colored pale brown, with spots. You will find this beautiful butterfly hard to miss as it flies around watercourses, shores, and backyards. Its caterpillars feed on legumes and crucifers. It is found in southern California, Arizona, Texas, and Florida and as far south as Argentina.

Species: *Urbanus proteus*
Family: Hesperiidae
1½–2 ins long
Flight period: Three or more
in Florida; from summer
to fall in the North

Northern Grizzled Skipper

Also called the Alpine Checkered Skipper. A checkered margin runs around the edges of this butterfly's wings, which are black with white spots. A look underneath the wings will reveal a brown-olive color, with light patches. You will find this butterfly in flowery meadows, glades, and clearings. It lays its eggs on rose plants. It is found from northern Alaska to Newfoundland, and south to the Carolinas.

♂♀   ♀

Species: *Pyrgus centaurea*
Family: Hesperiidae
1–1¼ ins long
Flight period: One, from April to August

♂♀   ♂

Species: *Lycaena helloides*
Family: Lycaenidae
1–1¼ ins long
Flight period: Continuous in southern California; from May to September elsewhere

Purplish Copper

Males of this butterfly have a purplish sheen on the wings and a broad, dark edge. Female wings are orange, copper, and brown with black marks. A look underneath the wings shows an orange-yellow color with black spots in both males and females. Look in meadows and alongside streams for this butterfly, from the sea right up to the mountains. Caterpillars, green with yellow stripes, feed on knotweeds, sorrels, and docks. It is found from the Arctic Circle to Baja California, and east to the Great Lakes.

Clouded Skipper

This butterfly's pointed wings are dark brown with a row of tiny white spots on the forewings. Underneath, the forewings have a violet color on them, and the hindwings have clouds of light and dark purple. The Clouded Skipper flies around grassy areas, waysides, and by streams. It has white and brown caterpillars. Their favorite food includes wooly beard-grass, St. Augustine grass, Indian corn, water grass, and paspalum. It is found from Illinois east to Massachusetts, south to Florida, west to Texas, and south to Central America.

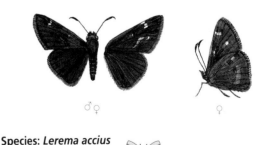

♂♀   ♀

Species: *Lerema accius*
Family: Hesperiidae
1–1½ ins long
Flight period: Several, from February to November in the South

Little Wood Satyr

This brown butterfly has two black eyespots on each wing, both above and below. The spots have yellow rims. There are clear darker brown lines crossing the wings underneath. The Little Wood Satyr likes any grassy, woody area. Its brown caterpillars feed on grasses and sedges. It is found in the eastern half of the U.S. and into southeastern Canada.

Species: *Megisto cymela*
Family: Satyridae
1³/₄–2 ins long
Flight period: One, from May to September

Zebra Swallowtail

This butterfly is an easy one to spot. It does not just have black and white stripes like a zebra, but red stripes, too. The red stripe is on the hindwing, along with red spots close to the body, and blue spots along the bottom. Other features that make the Zebra Swallowtail stand out are its triangular wings, and its very long, sharp-looking tails, on each hindwing. It likes to fly around meadows, and near water on riversides, and marshes. Its black and yellow striped caterpillars feed on pawpaw. It is found in southeastern U.S. north to New York.

Species: *Eurytides marcellus*
Family: Papilionidae
2¹/₂–3¹/₂ ins long
Flight period: From March to December

Brown Arctic

True to its name, this butterfly has light orange-brown wings. Small black eyespots can be seen on forewings and hindwings. The males have a darker patch across their wings. You may find this butterfly in a variety of places, but it prefers grassy areas. Caterpillars, which have olive, green, and brown stripes, like to feed on grasses. It is found from Alaska to Newfoundland, south to New Mexico and California.

Species: *Oeneis chryxus*
Family: Satyridae
1³/₄–2 ins long
Flight period: One, from May to August

Common Alpine

The dark brown wings of this butterfly are rounded, and have orange patches on forewings and hindwings. Inside these patches are black eyespots with white pupils. You may see the Common Alpine in several types of habitats, but it prefers grassy areas. The caterpillars have green stripes, and feed on grasses. It is found from Alaska to Manitoba and south to New Mexico.

Species:
Erebia epipsodea
Family: Satyridae
1³/₄–2 ins long
Flight period: One, from June to August

Streamside Checkerspot

Also called the Silvery Checkerspot. Look for a mainly dark brown butterfly with orange and yellow marks, and you have found the Streamside Checkerspot. Underneath, the hindwings have yellow, orange, and whitish marks, often with a silvery sheen. This butterfly lives around meadows and woods, as well as by streams. The black and orange-striped caterpillars have spines and feed on asters, coneflowers, and crownbeards. It is found in southern Canada and most of southeastern U.S.

Species: *Chlosyne nycteis*
Family: Nymphalidae – 1¹⁄₂–1³⁄₄ ins long
Flight period: Several, from March to September

Buckeye

You will have no trouble identifying this butterfly. It has four eyespots: two on each forewing, and two on each hindwing. Each eyespot is black, with a yellow rim. The background color is brown, and there are orange markings on each wing. Look for the Buckeye flying in meadows, and along roadsides and railroad embankments. Its caterpillars are dark colored with orange and yellow markings. They munch on lots of different plants, including plantain, figwort, and stonecrop. It is found throughout the South, going as far north as Southeast Canada.

Species: *Precis coenia*
Family: Nymphalidae
2–2¹⁄₂ ins long
Flight period: Two to four, continuous in the South; elsewhere, from March to October

Milbert's Tortoise Shell

Look at the bright orange bands which cross this butterfly's wings. Can you see why its other name is the Fire-rim? The outside margins are dark, and on the hindwing, these have a row of blue spots on the inside. The forewings have red patches going toward the body, and the rest of the wings are chocolate-brown. Underneath, they are dull brown and tan. This butterfly flies around waysides, roads, meadows, and streams. Caterpillars, black and spiny with green side stripes, feed on nettles. It is found from Alaska to Newfoundland, southwest to California and New Mexico.

Species: *Aglais milberti*
Family: Nymphalidae
1³⁄₄–2 ins long
Flight period: Three, from May to August

Large Wood Nymph

As its name suggests, this is a large butterfly. Mostly a chocolate-brown color, the wings have large black eyespots, which often lie in a band of orange-yellow. Underneath, the hindwing may have up to six eyespots on a mottled brown background. You may have trouble spotting the Large Wood Nymph as it perches on tree trunks in woodlands, well camouflaged against the bark. It also flies along waysides and in grassy areas. Caterpillars, green with yellow lines, feed on grasses. It is found in most of the U.S.except for the Southwest and in southern Canada.

Species: *Cercyonis pegala*
Family: Satyridae
2–3 ins long
Flight period: One, from June to September

Meadows & Grasslands

Little Glassy Wing

This is a brown butterfly with glassy white spots on both sides of the forewings. The spots are hard to miss and give the butterfly its name. Underneath, the hindwings are darker than above, with yellowish spots. The Little Glassywing flies in old meadows, pastures, grassy damp places in wooded areas and waysides. Its caterpillars, which are tan or green with dark stripes, feed on desert bunchgrass. It is found in Michigan east to New England, south to Georgia, Texas, and Nebraska.

Species: *Pompeius verna*
Family: Hesperiidae – 1–1¼ ins long
Flight period: One or more, from April to August

Hoary Edge

This butterfly has triangular wings which are blackish brown in color. There are glassy, yellow-gold marks on the forewings, and checkered margins all around the wings. The name "Hoary Edge" comes from the big white area which is underneath the hindwing, which looks like hoar frost. Look for this butterfly on woodland edges, in backyards, and meadows. Its caterpillars eat several types of legumes. It is found in Minnesota east to New Hampshire and south to Florida and north Texas.

Species: *Achalarus lyciades*
Family: Hesperiidae
1½–1¾ ins long
Flight period: One in the north, from May to July; many in the south, from April to December

Eastern Cloudy Wing

Also called the Southern Cloudy Wing. This butterfly's wings are brown, with lighter, checkered edges. The forewings have pale cream marks on them, which are joined together in bars. You can see it flying through clearings, in dry meadows, and on roadsides. The caterpillars eat different types of legumes. It is found in Minnesota and Nebraska, east to New England, south to Texas and Florida.

Species: *Thorybes bathyllus*
Family: Hesperiidae
1¼–1¾ ins long
Flight period: One in the north in June; two in the south from March to December

Long Dash

Both male and female Long Dashes have wings with orange markings in the middle, and a brown border around the outsides. Males have a long black mark almost to the edge of their forewings which gives the butterfly its name. Female forewings look different because they have yellow marks. The Long Dash flies in meadows and waysides, where its caterpillars feed on grasses, including bluegrass. It is found almost coast to coast in southern Canada and the U.S., except for British Columbia coast, and Washington State.

Species: *Polites mystic*
Family: Hesperiidae
1–1¼ ins long
Flight period: One, from May to September

Northern Dimorphic Skipper

Also called the Hobomok Skipper. Males and females of this butterfly usually have brown wings with pale yellow patches on the forewings. Males have a dark brand on their forewings, too. Sometimes the females look completely different and have yellow-orange colored wings. That is what "dimorphic" means. Underneath the hindwings of males and females is a yellowish patch. Look for this butterfly flying in grassy areas, such as meadows and clearings. Its caterpillars, which are dark green or brown with black spines, feed on grasses. It is found from Saskatchewan to Nova Scotia, and south to Georgia.

Species: *Poanes hobomok*
Family: Hesperiidae
1–1½ ins long
Flight period: One, from May to September

Holarctic Grass Skipper

Also called the Common Branded Skipper, this little butterfly has brownish wings with tawny-orange patches. Males can be recognized by the black mark on their forewings. Underneath, the wings are mottled green and yellow, with a curve of white spots. This butterfly lives in grassy areas, including meadows, foothills, and glades. Caterpillars feed on various grasses, including pine bluegrass and red fescue. It is found in Alaska south to Baja California and across to Newfoundland.

Species: *Hesperia comma*
Family: Hesperiidae
1 ins long
Flight period: One, from June to August

Swarthy Skipper

This is a small butterfly with no pattern on its dark brown wings. The forewings are a triangular shape, but the hindwings are rounded. Underneath, the wings are chestnut-colored, with yellow veins on the hindwings. The Swarthy Skipper can be spotted in fields, beaches, and meadows. Its caterpillars feed on prairie beard-grass. It is found from Maine to Florida and east to the Mississippi River.

Species: *Nastra lherminier* – **Family:** Hesperiidae
About 1 ins long – **Flight period:** Two, from June to September

Prairie Skipper

Also known as the Ottoe Skipper, this butterfly's wings are tawny brown with light brown margins. Males have a clear black mark on their forewings. The underside of the wings is similar to above, but with lighter markings. Look for this butterfly in grassy areas and prairies. It lays eggs on purple coneflower in Minnesota. When they hatch, the caterpillars feed on various grasses, including fall witchgrass. It is found in the central U.S. into southern Canada.

Species: *Hesperia ottoe*
Family: Hesperiidae
1¼–1¾ ins long
Flight period: One, from June to July

Golden-banded Skipper

It's easy to see the broad, golden bars against a black background that give this butterfly its name. There is also a white spot near the tip of each forewing. Around the edge of each hindwing is a checkered fringe. You can see this big butterfly at watersides, and in grassy areas and woodlands. Its caterpillars feed on hog peanut in Maryland. It is found from Ohio to New York, south to north Florida, Alabama, southeast Missouri, Gulf States, west Texas, southwest New Mexico, and southeast Arizona south into Mexico.

Species: *Autochton cellus*
Family: Hesperiidae
1³/₄–2 ins long

Flight period: Two in north, from May to August; more in the south, from February to September

Eastern Sedge Skipper

Also known as the Palmetto Skipper. This butterfly has rounded wings. Males have orange forewings with a brown margin, and females' forewings are brown with a row of orange spots. Both males and females have brown hindwings with a bright orange "ray" going toward the margin. An agile butterfly, it flutters around swamps, marshes, and bogs which have sedges and tall grasses. The caterpillars feed on lake sedge and wool grass. It is found in Wisconsin and Ontario, south to Texas and northern Florida.

Species: *Euphyes dion*
Family: Hesperiidae
1¹/₄–1³/₄ ins long
Flight period: One, from July to August in New Jersey

Blazing Star Skipper

Also called the Leonardus Skipper. Males are not as dark as the females of this butterfly. They have orange markings on their wings, with a dark brown border. Females are all dark brown except for some pale orange bands on each wing. Underneath, the hindwings are chestnut with a row of white spots. This butterfly lives in fields and meadows, prairies, and clearings. Caterpillars, which are maroon with green marks, feed on bent grass, panic grass, and tumble grass. It is found in central U.S. and southern Canada to the East Coast.

Species: *Hesperia leonardus*
Family: Hesperiidae – 1–1¹/₂ ins long

Flight period: One, from August to October

Yellow-patch Skipper

This butterfly is so-called because it has yellow-orange patches on its wings, which are also brown and orange. Females, which are bigger than the males, are a little darker in color. Underneath, the hindwings have pale yellow bands. Look for it in grassy open spaces, meadows, and prairies. Its caterpillars feed on grasses. It is found from coast to coast in the U.S., except the West Coast area of British Columbia and Oregon.

Species: *Polites coras* – Family: Hesperiidae
³/₄–1 ins long

Flight period: One, from May to September

Indian Skipper

You will notice this butterfly because of its long, triangular wings patterned with orange and brown. Underneath, the wings are orange and tan, and the hindwings have a band of pale spots. The Indian Skipper flies in fields and meadows, and can be spotted in early springtime. Caterpillars, which are reddish brown with light speckles, feed on different types of grasses. It is found in southern Ontario east to Maine, south to Virginia and Tennessee, and west to Wisconsin and Iowa.

Species: *Hesperia sassacus*
Family: Hesperiidae
1–1½ ins long
Flight period: One, from May to July

Least Skipperling

A small butterfly, with rounded wings, the Least Skipperling is orange and black, with more orange on the hindwings. Underneath, the wings are a bright orange-gold. With its distinctive two-toned wings, this butterfly is easy to spot flying around grasses in the meadows, pastures, and marshes where it lives. It has light green caterpillars that munch on marsh millet, bluegrass, and rice. It is found in most of eastern U.S. to west of the Mississippi, and southern and eastern Canada.

Species: *Ancyloxypha numitor*
Family: Hesperiidae
¾–1 ins long
Flight period: Several, from February to December

Arctic Skipperling

This butterfly has warm brown wings with rich orange markings. Underneath, the hindwings are yellow-orange with several yellow blotches. The Arctic Skipperling is well known in many countries. It flies around waysides and grassy areas where it sips nectar from wild iris flowers. Its caterpillars, which are dusky green, feed on purple reedgrass. It is found from the East to West Coasts across the northern part of the U.S.

Species: *Carterocephalus palaemon*
Family: Hesperiidae – ¾–1¼ ins long
Flight period: One, from May to July

Plains Yucca Giant Skipper

The other name for this butterfly, Strecker's Giant Skipper, comes from a 19th-century butterfly expert called Strecker. Large and broad-winged, this butterfly is easy to spot. It has dark brown wings with yellow spots, and white marks at the tips of the forewings. Underneath, the forewings look similar, but the hindwings are gray-brown with some white spots. It likes to fly around prairies and open woodlands, and yucca plains. Caterpillars feed on the root of yucca plants. It is found from Montana to Texas and east to Nevada.

Species: *Megathymus streckeri* – **Family:** Hesperiidae
2–3 ins long – **Flight period:** One, from May to July

Raising Butterflies

A good way to learn more about butterflies is to rear them yourself, from caterpillars. Look for caterpillars in the spring and summer on leaves, stems, and grasses. It is very important that your caterpillars have enough food, otherwise they will starve to death.

It's easy to find the right food—just make a note of where you found the caterpillar and what the plant was, so you can return and collect more when you need it. (Take a stalk of the plant with some leaves if you are not sure you will recognize it again.)

Rearing cages

Caterpillar-rearing cages are available from special stores, otherwise you can easily make your own. You could use:

- a card shoebox covered with window screening on top
- a sheet of clear plastic rolled into a tube standing in a plastic tub with soil in the bottom
- a large clear jar (2 pints or more)

For the last two, cover the top with cheesecloth and secure it with an elastic band.

How to rear caterpillars

1 **When you have found some caterpillars, break off the piece of the plant** you found them on and gently place it in your prepared container. When the caterpillars are newly hatched and tiny, they don't need a big cage. A jar or plastic box lined with newspaper will do.
2 **Remember that your caterpillars will need new leaves EVERY day.**
3 **When they grow bigger** (after their first molt,) you will need to transfer the caterpillars to a more suitable container (see above.) Be careful! Move your caterpillars using the tip of a small paintbrush. This will help you to avoid damaging them, and it also stops them damaging you (some caterpillars have stinging hairs.) Place them on their food plant in the new cage.

4 **Now you can pick bigger bits of the food plant, and place them in a jar of water to keep them fresh.** Put a twig or stick in too, for perching, and for the caterpillars to hang their chrysalises from. Make sure you plug up the top of the jar with cotton to stop the growing caterpillars from falling in. Keep putting fresh plants in every other day.

5 **Caterpillars may take a while to turn into chrysalises**—and sometimes they have to spend the winter in the chrysalis. If they go very still, leave them alone in a cool place until spring.

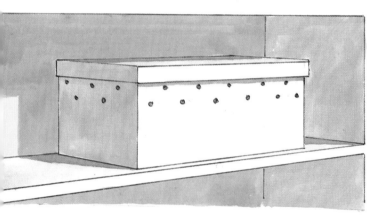

6 **Remember to label the caterpillars' or pupae's box** with the date, species name, etc.
7 **If the caterpillars pupate in soil or sand, spray the soil occasionally with water** as it must be damp—otherwise the pupae might die.

8 **When the adult butterflies have struggled out of the chrysalis,** remove the top of the cage and put it outside. They will only fly away when their wings have dried and expanded.

What to watch for

When you are rearing your caterpillars, make notes of the following things. Also, try sketching the different stages in the butterfly's life as they occur.
- What is the name of the food plant you found your caterpillars on?
- How many times do the caterpillars molt?
- Do any of the caterpillars make a leaf tent?
- How long do the caterpillars take to turn into chrysalises?
- What are the chrysalises like? Can you see the butterfly's wings through the skin, and at what stage?
- How long does it take for the butterfly to break out of the chrysalis skin?
- How long does it take the butterfly to dry? And to pump up its wings?
- Can you identify the butterfly?

Grasshopper Satyr

Also known as Riding's Satyr, the Grasshopper Satyr gets its usual name because its patterns are like those on a grasshopper. You will have no problem identifying this butterfly, as no other American butterfly has such a color or pattern. Different shades of gray cover its wings, while creamy colored bands cross them from top to bottom. There are several black eyespots with white pupils on each forewing. Underneath, the wings are a speckled gray. Caterpillars are reddish with green bands, and feed on grasses. It is found in Alberta and Saskatchewan, south to Arizona and New Mexico.

Species: *Neominois ridingsii*
Family: Satyridae
1½–2 ins long
Flight period: Two, from June to August

Gray Copper

Also called the Great Gray Copper, because of its large size. Both males and females of this butterfly have gray wings, as the name suggests. Females are a bit smaller than the males, and have more orange marks than the males around the margin of their hindwings. There are some black markings on the wings of both males and females. It might be difficult to watch this butterfly, as it flies quite jerkily. Wait until it stops to drink nectar from milkweed in the meadows and prairies in which it lives. Caterpillars may be green, yellow-green, or magenta with orange stripes. They munch on docks. It is found in the central and western U.S., and in southern Canada.

Species: *Lycaena xanthoides*
Family: Lycaenidae – 1¼–1¾ ins long
Flight period: One, from May to July

Northern Cloudy Wing

Rounded, brown wings with white marks on the forewings are the features of this butterfly. Checkered fringes run around the edges of the wings. The Northern Cloudy Wing is very common, and flies in open woods, roadsides, meadows, fields, and clearings. Its caterpillars feed on legumes, where they make silken nests. It is found from Northwest Territories to Florida and California.

Species: *Thorybes pylades*
Family: Hesperiidae
1¼–1¾ ins long
Flight period: Two, from March to December

Primrose Blue

Also called the High Mountain Blue. Males and females of this butterfly look similar. They have grayish brown wings. Underneath, the wings are brown with bright white markings and black spots. This butterfly flies in tundra and mountain meadows, prairies, and open woodland. Its caterpillars probably feed on rock jasmine and shooting star in the further south, and diapensia in the Arctic. They may also eat blueberry. It is found from California to Newfoundland and Greenland.

Species: *Plebejus glandon*
Family: Lycaenidae
¾–1 ins long
Flight period: One, from June to August

Wolf-face Sulfur

Also called the Mexican Yellow. Look for the long-snouted wolf's face on the dark forewing tip of this butterfly. The male has white wings with a yellow mark at the top of the hindwings, and the female has pale yellow wings. You may see this butterfly around meadows, desert chaparral, and mountain canyons. Caterpillars munch on senna plants. It is found in Mexico, Arizona, New Mexico, and as far north as Manitoba.

Species: *Eurema mexicana*
Family: Pieridae
1¹/₂–2 ins long
Flight period:
From March to
November

Western Orange Tip

Also called the Sara Orange Tip, it is easy to see how this butterfly got its name. It has bright orange tips on each of its forewings, surrounded by a black margin. Its coloring may be confusing, as males can be either white or yellow, but females are always yellow. A look underneath the hindwings will reveal a mottled grass-green color. It flies around meadows, mountain roads, by streams, and even in desert canyons. Its caterpillars are moss green, with white and darker green, too. They like to feed on many kinds of mustard plant. It is found from British Columbia to Mexico and New Mexico.

Species: *Anthocaris sara*
Family: Pieridae
1¹/₄–1³/₄ ins long
Flight period:
From February to July

Coral Hairstreak

Males and females of this butterfly look different. The male has very dark brown pointed wings, with light reddish spots on the hindwing margin. Females have rounded wings, which are lighter brown. They also sport red spots along the hindwing margin. Underneath, males and females are lighter brown with black spots rimmed with white, and bright orange spots all along the hindwing margin. The Coral Hairstreak flies rapidly through meadows, alighting on flowers to sip nectar and also in shrubby and wooded areas. Its yellow-green caterpillars feed on unripe plums and wild cherries. It is found across the U.S. and Canada, except the Pacific Coast, along the Gulf Coast and in Florida.

Species: *Harkenclenus titus*
Family: Lycaenidae
1–1¹/₄ ins long
Flight period: One, from June to August

Rosy Marble

Also known as the Olympia Marblewing. This chalky white butterfly has gray marks on its wings, and a rosy color both above and below the base of its hindwings. There is also a mottled green underneath the hindwing, which gives it good camouflage when it folds its wings against greenery. You may see this butterfly fluttering around open woods and meadows, as well as foothills and dunes. Caterpillars are bright green, striped with gray and yellow, and feed on buds and flowers of cress, and mustard plants. It is found in central U.S. and east into Virginia.

Species: *Euchloe olympia*
Family: Pieridae
1¹/₂–1³/₄ ins long
Flight period: One, from March to June

Ringlet

An orange-brown color on top, this butterfly has eyespots above and beneath its wings. The eyespots underneath are black and yellow rimmed, with white dots in the middle. You can spot the Ringlet in grassy areas. Caterpillars feed on grasses or sedges. It is found from Alaska to California to Newfoundland.

Species: *Coenonympha tullia*
Family: Satyridae
1–2 ins long
Flight period: Continuous, from May to September

Black-vein Skipper

Also known as the Delaware Skipper. Males and females of this butterfly have bright orange wings with dark borders and veins, but females are larger and darker, with darker veins and a wider border. Underneath, the wings are pale. You can spot it on the edges of woodlands, and in grassy areas. Caterpillars are black and white, and feed on different types of grasses. It is found in most of the U.S. east of the Mississippi, and southern Canada.

Species: *Atrytone logan*
Family: Hesperiidae
1–1½ ins long
Flight period: One, from February to October

Sachem

Both males and females of this butterfly have tawny orange and brown wings. However, it is easy to tell which ones are the males, as they have a huge black mark on their wings. Females can be recognized by the two bright spots they have on their forewings. Underneath, forewings are tawny, and hindwings are dusky yellow. Look out for the Sachem flying in pastures and fields, as well as in backyards. Lots of Sachems appear in the summertime. Its caterpillars feed on different types of grasses. It is found throughout the southern third of the U.S., and can also be seen in Oregon, Colorado, Iowa, and New York.

Species: *Atalopedes campestris*
Family: Hesperiidae
1–1½ ins long
Flight period: Three in the South, flies for most of the year

European Skipperling

This butterfly has dark orange wings with black veins towards the edges and a dark border. Underneath, the wings are yellowish green. The European Skipperling comes originally from Europe, but was brought to America in 1910. It flies around meadows and pastures, and its green caterpillars feed on timothy. It is found on the East Coast of the U.S. and Canada, spreading westward.

Species: *Thymelicus lineola*
Family: Hesperiidae
¾–1 ins long
Flight period: One, from June to August

Hairy Dusky Wing

Also known as the Persius Dusky Wing, this brownish black butterfly has tiny glass dots on its forewing tips. It is called "hairy" because males have long gray hair on their forewings. Hindwings of males and females have rows of black markings. Underneath, the wings are lighter brown. A fairly rare butterfly, the Hairy Dusky Wing flies in grasslands and open woodlands. Its caterpillars, which are light green and hairy, feed on lupine in the east, and golden banner in the west. It is found mostly in western Canada and U.S., some in the eastern part of the U.S.

Species: *Erynnis persius*
Family: Hesperiidae
1–1½ ins long
Flight period: Two,
from May to September

Mottled Arctic

Also called the Melissa Arctic. This tan-colored butterfly has no markings on top, but if you look underneath the hindwing you will see a dark gray mottled pattern. Its wings are almost transparent, so it is well camouflaged against lichen-covered rocks in the Arctic meadows in which it lives. The caterpillars of this butterfly are green with blue and spotted yellow stripes. They feed on grasses and sedges. It is found from Alaska to New Mexico across the north to Newfoundland.

Species: *Oeneis melissa*
Family: Satyridae – 1¾–2 ins long
Flight period: One, from June to August

Brown-rim Skipper

Another name for this butterfly is the Beard-grass Skipper. Males have tawny orange wings with dark brown margins, and females have broader margins on their wings, and not as much orange color. Underneath, the wings are lighter, sometimes even bright yellow. The Brown-rim Skipper lives in beard-grass fields, and lays its eggs there. When they are born, the caterpillars eat beard-grass. It is found in Minnesota east to New York, south to Florida, west to Texas, and north to Nebraska, Colorado, and Wyoming.

Species: *Atrytone arogos*
Family: Hesperiidae
1–1¼ ins long
Flight period: One in the
north, from June to July,
two in the south from
March to May and from
August to September

Banded Arctic

Also called the Polixenes Arctic. A look underneath this butterfly's hindwing will show you the reason for its name, as a broad dark band crosses the wing. Apart from this, the wings have no markings, and are a grayish brown, and almost transparent. This butterfly is hard to spot among the grassy areas in which it lives. Its caterpillars feed on arctic and alpine grasses. It is found in Alaska and Newfoundland south to New Mexico.

Species: *Oeneis polixenes*
Family: Satyridae
1½–1¾ ins long
Flight period: One,
from June to August

Variegated Fritillary

Orange-brown colors with busy black patterns of spots and stripes are the trademarks of this butterfly. Underneath the wings, the pattern continues, but it is fainter. Females of this butterfly are bigger than the males. The Variegated Fritillary likes to fly around open grassy areas, such as fields, grasslands, and meadows. Caterpillars, colored white with red bands and black spines, are not fussy about their diet. They will eat almost anything, from violets and pansies, to plantain and passion flower. It is found from the southern states to Canada.

Species: *Euptoieta claudia*
Family: Nymphalidae – 1³/₄–2¹/₄ ins long
Flight period: Continuous in the south; one, from March to December northward

Great Plains Checkerspot

Also called the Gorgone Checkerspot, this butterfly is orange, yellow, and brown, with a row of black spots on the hindwing. Underneath, the hindwing is gray with heavy black marks. It flutters around flowery meadows and waysides, as well as in woodlands. Caterpillars are orange-red with black bands, and feed on sunflowers, ragweed, sump-weed, and goldeneye. It is found from Alberta to Texas and Georgia.

Species: *Chlosyne gorgone*
Family: Nymphalidae
1¹/₄–1¹/₂ ins long
Flight period: One, from May to September

Meadow Fritillary

This butterfly has dark orange-brown wings with black dashes and dots. The male's forewing tip looks as if it has been cut off at a strange angle. Underneath the hindwing is orange-brown, gray, and lilac. The Meadow Fritillary can be spotted in damp meadows, or indeed near any marshy spot. Caterpillars, purplish black with brown spines, feed on violets. It is found from Yukon to Quebec and southeast to Georgia.

Species: *Boloria bellona*
Family: Nymphalidae
1¹/₄–2 ins long
Flight period: Three, from May to September

Small Copper

This butterfly has three different names: the Small Copper because of its small size, the American Copper because of where it lives, and the Flame Copper because of its bright fiery color. The forewings are a bright copper color on top with dark spots and a dark margin. Hindwings are brown with copper borders. Look in flowery meadows and on waste ground for this butterfly. Their caterpillars, which are green and rose-colored, feed on sheep sorrel and curly dock, or mountain sorrel. It is widely distributed even within the Arctic Circle.

Species: *Lycaena phlaeas*
Family: Lycaenidae
1–1¹/₄ ins long
Flight period: One or several, from April to October in the south.

Pearl Crescentspot

An orange color with dark margins around its wings and dark markings, this butterfly is also called the Pearly Crescentspot. Look for the white crescent-shaped marks along the hindwing borders. It likes to fly over meadows, fields, and prairies, quite near the ground. The males are quite cheeky, and will often dart out to investigate a passerby. Caterpillars are spiny and brown with yellow bands. They feed on the leaves of asters. It is found from Alberta to Maine, across the U.S. to Arizona.

Species: *Phyciodes tharos*
Family: Nymphalidae
1–1½ ins long
Flight period: Several, from April to August

Silver Meadow Fritillary

This is a small butterfly with black-marked orange wings. It is also called the Silver-bordered Fritillary because underneath its hindwing, you can see rows of metallic silver spots, including a row on the margin. True to its name, this butterfly likes meadows, but can also be seen around bogs, near woodlands, or among plains. Its caterpillars are brownish black with yellow spines, and feed on violets. It is found from Alaska to Newfoundland, and south to New Mexico.

Species: *Boloria selene*
Family: Nymphalidae
1½–2 ins long
Flight period: Three, from May to October

Field Crescentspot

This butterfly is blackish brown, speckled with orange and yellow patches and spots. Underneath, the forewing is pale orange, while the hindwing is pale tan. Females are a little larger than the males. This is the Crescentspot you are most likely to see, as it is the commonest one in North America. Look for it flying about meadows, forest clearings, and swamps and fields. Its spiny, blackish brown caterpillars feed on aster leaves. It is found from Alaska to New Mexico.

Species: *Phyciodes campestris* – Family: Nymphalidae
1¼–1½ ins long – Flight period: Four, from April to October

Great Spangled Fritillary

This butterfly is so called because of the silver spangles underneath the hindwing. It is orange-brown, with dark patterns of dots, dashes, and crescents. The black marks get darker towards the body. Look for the Great Spangled Fritillary flying swiftly, pausing to drink nectar from flowers. It flies around meadows and woodland glades. You will find the caterpillars, which are tiny with black spines, feeding on violets. It is found from the East to the West Coasts of the U.S, and in southern Canada.

Species:
Speyeria cybele
Family:
Nymphalidae
2¼–3 ins long
Flight period:
One, from
June to September

Meadows & Grasslands

Pink-edged Sulfur

Yellow wings and bright pink fringes are the trademarks of this butterfly. You can tell the male by the thick black borders on its wings. Females have little or no border. There is an orange spot on each hindwing of both males and females. Look around flowery meadows, woodlands, and also marshes and bogs for this butterfly. Its caterpillars are bright yellow-green with lighter back stripes, and feed on blueberries. It is found from Oregon to Newfoundland.

Species: *Colias interior* – **Family:** Pieridae
1½–1¾ ins long
Flight period: One, from June to August

Common Sulfur

Males of this type of butterfly are always yellow with a thick black border, but females are sometimes white, with a yellow-spotted black border. Both males and females have an orange spot in the middle of each hindwing. Underneath, they are a greenish yellow color. Look for the Common Sulfur in flowery meadows, pastures, forests, and deserts. Its caterpillars are bright green and feed on clovers. It is found in most of the U.S. and Canada, except for the tip of Florida.

Species: *Colias philodice*
Family: Pieridae – 1½–1¾ ins long
Flight period: Two to three,
from March to December

Species: *Eurema lisa*
Family: Pieridae
1–1½ ins long
Flight period: Continuous, from
May to October in the north.

Little Sulfur

It is also called the Little Yellow, from its yellow color. A good way of recognizing this butterfly is by its small size, often smaller than your little finger. Its wings have black borders, which are stronger in the males. Females are often paler yellow than males. They fly around open areas, like roadsides and fields. Caterpillars are green with white stripes, and feed on senna, partridge pea, clovers, and hog peanut. It is found in the southwestern U.S., north to the Great Lakes, and west to Mexico.

Black-dust Skipper

Also known as the Green Skipper. This butterfly is orange, with wide brown borders. Females are brighter in color than males. Underneath, the forewings are similar, but the hindwings are bright olive-green. There are also white spots underneath. This butterfly lives in prairies and canyons. The caterpillars feed on grass. It is found from Wyoming and Nebraska south to west Texas, east Arizona, and Mexico.

Species: *Hesperia viridis*
Family: Hesperiidae
1–1½ ins long
Flight period: Two, from
April to June and from
August to October

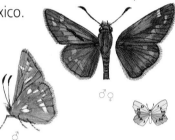

♂♀

♂

Southern Dimorphic Skipper

Also called the Zabulon Skipper. Males of this butterfly are yellow-orange above and below, with brown spots underneath. Females are black, with a violet tinge under their wings. This butterfly flies around grassy areas such as meadows and scrubland. It often sips nectar from violets. The caterpillars feed on grasses, including tumble grass. It is found in Wisconsin east to Massachusetts, south to Georgia, Texas, and Panama.

Species: *Poanes zabulon*
Family: Hesperiidae
1–1½ ins long
Flight period: Two,
from May to August

♂♀

♂

Fiery Skipper

This butterfly gets its name from its bright yellow-orange color. Males have patterned wings with a zigzagged border, and females have long wings and large orange spots. Both males and females have very short feelers. The Fiery Skipper lives in grassy areas such as clearings, waysides, and forest edges. Its caterpillars feed on grasses. It is found in North and South Dakota, south through Colorado and Kansas to New Mexico and Arizona.

Species: *Hylephila phyleus*
Family: Hesperiidae
1–1¼ ins long
Flight period: Two or more,
from April to December in south California

♂♀

Ultraviolet Sulfur

Also known as Queen Alexandra's Sulfur, after Queen Alexandra of England. The male of this type of butterfly is bright lemon-yellow with a thick black border on its wings. The female can be yellow or white, and does not usually have the black border. Both males and females have a black spot on each forewing. Underneath, the hindwings are green, with a silvery spot. This butterfly can be seen around clearings, meadows, and roadsides. The caterpillars, colored green with lengthwise stripes, feed on vegetable plants, including wild pea. It is found in the Rocky Mountains and the Great Plains.

Species: *Colias alexandra*
Family: Pieridae
1½–2 ins long
Flight period: One,
from June to July

♂♀

Butterfly Garden

If you have a garden, you can do a lot to make it attractive to butterflies. This will not only help the butterflies, it will also make your yard a very colorful place. The best way to start is to grow flowers that have lots of nectar. Many butterflies love to sip this with their long tongues, which are a bit like straws. Trees, too, can attract butterflies—some species like to drink tree sap, or eat rotten fruit on the ground.

Don't forget about the caterpillars—if you grow their food plants, it will encourage female butterflies to lay their eggs there. Another important thing to remember is not to use poison sprays in your garden. These can kill butterflies as well as pests.

Butterfly watching

Watching how butterflies and caterpillars behave in the field can be interesting and exciting. You can get a really good look at them if they are busy feeding or drinking, so a flowery garden is one of the best places to start. Approach the butterfly quietly and be careful not to make any sudden movements—this will frighten it away.

Caterpillars can't fly away, but they can look like something else—such as leaves, twigs, or even bird droppings. You'll need to look extra carefully for these. Beware of hairy caterpillars—they can give you a nasty rash.

Flowers & trees

Adult butterflies will feed on lots of different flowers. Most prefer certain colors like pink, mauve, and purple. Large butterflies prefer to feed from tall flowers, while smaller types like low-growing flowers. Butterflies also like flowers with flat tops or large petals that are easy to land on. If you let a piece of your garden go wild, the wild

flowers and weeds that grow there will also attract butterflies.

Nettles: Red Admirals lay their eggs on nettles, as this is their caterpillars' food plant.

Daisies: Don't get rid of your daisies—butterflies like the Western Skipper sip their nectar.

Clover: These are food plants for many types of caterpillars.

Other good flowering plants are sunflowers, lilacs, passion flowers, pansies, marigolds, and rock roses.

Buddleia: The flowers that this shrub produces are so popular with butterflies that it is often called the butterfly bush. The Pipevine Swallowtail is an example of a buddleia-loving butterfly.

The leaves of trees are food plants for many types of caterpillars. Favorite trees include: oak, birch, willow, sycamore, walnut, cherry, and poplar.

When is a butterfly not a butterfly?

When it's a moth, of course! There are even more moths than butterflies around (more than 87,000 species worldwide,) but as a general rule, they are not so noticeable. This is the way you tell them apart, but remember there are exceptions to all these tests:

- Butterflies fly during the day; moths fly at night.
- Butterflies are brightly colored; moths are usually drably colored.
- Butterflies rest with their wings held vertically; moths rest with them held flat.
- The antennae of most butterflies end in small clubs (see page 6.)

Deserts & Mountains

Hot, dry, sandy deserts do not seem like suitable places for butterflies, but many live there all the same. Don't expect to see butterflies during the hottest time of the day though—they usually shelter from the heat of the midday sun, venturing out when it is cooler—early in the morning, or late in the evening.

There are two main deserts in North America, and both are in the West. The Great Basin runs through Nevada. Southwest of this, in California, is the Mojave Desert. The best places to look for butterflies is near plants, or around water holes.

High up in the clouds, often wind-swept and cold, mountains also seem like unlikely butterfly homes. And it is true that the butterflies that live here have to be hardy. The weather often changes quickly from sunny and tranquil to windy and snowy. When the sun is out, mountain butterflies make the most of it: they sunbathe with their wings outstretched. They often have dark-colored wings to absorb the heat quickly. Hairy bodies also help to keep in the precious warmth should the weather change suddenly. Notice the way that butterflies of these areas fly—close to the ground and in short bursts. This is to combat the fierce winds that often sweep over mountain tops. This picture shows seven species from this section; how many can you recognize?

Northern Blue; Orange Hairstreak; Western Willow Hairstreak; Yucca Giant Skipper; Dainty Sulfur; Short-tailed Black Swallowtail; Checkered White.

Western Willow Hairstreak

Also called the Sylvan Hairstreak. Males look slightly different from the females of this butterfly. They have light brown wings, while the females are darker and grayish. Both males and females have some reddish color near the base of their hindwings. They usually have tails, but, confusingly, some of these butterflies are tailless. Underneath, the wings are gray to white-gray. This butterfly can be seen near willow trees, which is their caterpillars' favorite foodplant. It is found in British Columbia to Baja California and east to New Mexico.

Species: *Satyrium sylvinus*
Family: Lycaenidae
1–1¼ ins long
**Flight period: One,
from May to August**

Mesquite Metalmark

Also called the Grey Metalmark, from the honey mesquite plant that its caterpillars eat in the desert. If you spot this plant, the butterflies should be nearby! The Grey Metalmark is a small butterfly, with a gray-brown background on its wings, covered with white and orange spots and dashes, which give a bright pattern. It is found from southern California to west Texas.

Species: *Apodemia palmerii*
Family: Lycaenidae
¾–1 ins long
**Flight period: Three,
from April to November**

Redhead Sooty Wing

Also called the Goldenheaded Sooty Wing because of its orange head, this butterfly is otherwise dull in color. Its wings, which are very rounded, are dark brown, both on top, and underneath. It flies in canyons, at the bottom of valleys, and in foothills. It is found in southern New Mexico, southern Arizona, west and south Texas and northern Mexico.

Species: *Staphylus ceos*
Family: Hesperiidae
1–1¼ ins long
**Flight period: Several,
from spring and fall**

Columbine Dusky Wing

A small butterfly, the Columbine Dusky Wing gets its name from the wild columbine plants that its caterpillar eats. It has short, rounded wings, which are dark, with little spots on the forewings and bands of darker marks. The hindwings are plain dark brown. You will see this butterfly on the edges of woodlands, in glades, and in upland areas. It is found from Manitoba to the East Coast, and south to the Carolinas.

Species: *Erynnis lucilus*
Family: Nymphalidae
1–1¼ ins long
**Flight period: Two or three,
from May to August**

White-veined Skipper

Also called the Uncas Skipper, this butterfly is tawny brown with yellow marks on the forewing. You can spot the males by the black mark they have on the forewings. Look underneath, and the forewing is similar. The hindwing underside has several silver marks and white veins, hence the name. Its caterpillars feed on needle grass and blue grama grass growing in the grassland areas where this butterfly lives. It is found in central and western U.S. and in southern Canada.

Species:
Hesperia uncas
Family:
Hesperiidae
1–1³/4 ins long
Flight period: Two or more, from May to September

Yucca Giant Skipper

A large butterfly, the Yucca Giant Skipper has black wings with yellow marks and borders. A good identification mark to look for is the white spot at the top of the forewings. Another feature is the big, plump body, which is black or dark brown. Look for this butterfly in deserts, scrubby woodlands, and old fields. As the name suggests, its caterpillars feed on yucca plants. Here, they make silk shelters by strapping some leaves together. It is found east to west across the U.S.

Species: *Megathymus yuccae*
Family: Hesperiidae
2–2³/4 ins long
Flight period: One, from January to June

Cliff Swallowtail

This butterfly is also known as the Short-tailed Black Swallowtail because it has shorter "tails" than most swallowtails. Its wings are mainly black, with pale yellow spots and bands. There are faint blue markings on the hindwings, along with orange eyespots. You may spot this butterfly around mountains, canyons, and cliffs, where males often take part in exciting flight displays, battering each other in the air in competition for a territory or a mate. The caterpillars, often colored black and white, feed on carrot or parsley plants. It is found on the West Coast of the U.S., east to Wyoming.

Species: *Papilio indra*
Family: Papilionidae
2¹/4–3¹/2 ins long
Flight period: One to two northward, from May to July

Deserts & Mountains

Western Tiger Swallowtail

Above and below, this butterfly is lemon-yellow, with black tiger stripes across its wings, and thick black margins with yellow spots. You can also see orange and blue markings at the base of its hindwings. You will probably spot this butterfly in the western states, as it rarely flies east of the Rockies. Look out for big groups of males gathered around mud puddles or beside streams. Green caterpillars feed on trees such as willows, poplars, and sycamores. It is found from British Columbia south to Baja California, and east to New Mexico.

Species: *Pterourus rutulus*
Family: Papilionidae
2³/₄–4 ins long
Flight period: From February to November

Orange Hairstreak

Named for its orange wings, this butterfly may also be called Behr's Hairstreak. The wings have dark margins at the edges. Underneath, the wings are gray with rows of black and white speckles.
This butterfly likes dry areas, and you will probably be able to get quite close before it flies away. The caterpillar, green with white, yellow, or dark green stripes, feeds on antelope brush. It is near this plant that you are most likely to see the butterflies. It is found from British Columbia to New Mexico and California.

Species: *Satyrium behrii*
Family: Lycaenidae
1–1¹/₄ ins long
Flight period: One, from June to July

Dainty Sulfur

The tiny size of this butterfly has earned it this, and its other name, Dwarf Yellow. Both males and females have yellow wings, with dark forewing tips, which are stronger on the female. The female may also have an orangy color on the hindwings. Underneath, the wings are greenish yellow to gray, with black spots. Look for the Dainty Sulphur in waysides and canyons, or flying along rivers or railroad tracks. Caterpillars, a deep green color with purple back stripes, feed on weeds, marigolds, and daisies. It is found in Southern California, Arizona, and Gulf States, south into Mexico. It emigrates most years throughout Midwest to Manitoba.

Species: *Nathalis iole*
Family: Pieridae
³/₄–1¹/₄ ins long
Flight period:
Any month in the south; later farther north

♂♀

♀

Crossline Skipper

You can tell the male Crossline Skippers from the females by their pointed forewings, which also have a thin dark line crossing them. Both males and females have orange-brown wings. Underneath, the wings are dull brown, with spots on the hindwing. You can see this butterfly in canyons as well as in dry meadows, open woodland, and prairies. Its dark brown, black-headed caterpillars feed on desert bunchgrass. It is found in most of the eastern U.S., except southern Florida.

Species:
Polites origenes
Family: Hesperiidae
1–1¼ ins long
Flight period:
One, from June
to August

Black-veined Skipperling

Above, the wings of this butterfly are bright orange, with black veins. Underneath, the wings are light yellow to reddish gold, and there is a yellow "ray" on the hindwing that gives this butterfly its other name, the Sunrise Skipperling. It can be spotted in dry areas such as deserts and scrubland, near sources of water such as springs. It is found in western Texas and southeast Arizona south to Mexico.

Species: *Adopaeoides prittwitzi*
Family: Hesperiidae
1–1¼ ins long
Flight period: Two,
from May to June,
and in September

♂♀

Yellow-dust Skipper

This butterfly, also called the Pahaska Skipper, is orange with a brown border round its wings. There is a yellow dusting on the forewings, which gives it the name. Underneath, the forewing looks similar to above, but the hindwing is brownish with silver-white spots. This butterfly is fond of grassy areas and canyons, and its caterpillars feed on grasses. It is found on the east side of the Rockies, from Saskatchewan to Nevada and California.

♂♀

Species: *Hesperia pahaska*
Family: Hesperiidae
1¼–1½ ins long
Flight period: Two, from May to September

Arrowhead Skipper

Also called Morrison's Silver Spike from its discoverer H.K. Morrison. This butterfly's forewings are a tawny orange, with dark borders. The hindwings are brown, and make a dog's head pattern. Underneath, the forewings are similar, but the hindwings are rust-brown, crossed by silvery marks, which together, look like an arrowhead. This butterfly lives in mountain valleys and moist meadows, pine forests, foothills and hilltops. It is found in Colorado, New Mexico, Arizona, and West Texas.

♂♀

Species: *Stinga morrisoni*
Family: Hesperiidae
1–1¼ ins long
Flight period: One, from
May to mid-June in the Rockies,
but later farther south

♀

Deserts & Mountains

Spring White

You will be able to tell this butterfly from other Whites because it is so small in comparison. It has brownish markings around the edges of the forewings, and gray veins on the underside of the hindwings. A hardy butterfly, it can be found from lowlands to mountains, from freezing cold to very hot temperatures. Its caterpillars, which have black and yellow stripes, feed on rock cress, jewel flower, and different types of mustard plants. It is found from the Yukon to Baja California and east to Dakota.

Species: *Pontia sisymbrii*
Family: Pieridae
1¼–1½ ins long
Flight period: One, from February to July

Checkered White

Against a white background, this butterfly has dark checkering that gives it its name. Females have more dark marks than the males. Underneath, the hindwings are an olive green color. The types you will see in the summer are paler than those found in the spring. Males are almost completely white at this time. The Checkered White lives around lowland open spaces, especially in wastelands and weedy plots. Caterpillars are blue-green with black speckles. They feed on many types of mustard plants, bee plants, and capers. It is found in almost all of the U.S. and Mexico and southern Canada.

Species: *Pontia protodice*
Family: Pieridae
1¼–1¾ ins long
Flight period: From March to October

Western White

This butterfly has black and white checkered wings, with olive green scales underneath the hindwings. Females have more markings than the males. The Western White lives around lowlands such as clearings and fields, but also flies high up mountains in the Arctic. Caterpillars are green with light and dark bands, and feed on mustard plants. It is found from Alaska to New Mexico.

Species:
Pontia occidentalis
Family: Pieridae
1¼–1¾ ins long
Flight period:
Two, from April to September

Pale Crescent

Called the Pale or Pallid Crescentspot because of its light-brown color, this butterfly has a few dark marks on its wings. Its wing margins look sculptured, and the forewing is indented sharply. You will find it flying around foothills, valleys, canyons, and washes. Females lay their eggs on thistles, and the caterpillars, which are ocher with brown stripes and spines, feed on thistle plants. It is found from British Columbia to New Mexico.

Species: *Phyciodes pallida*
Family: Nymphalidae
1¼–1¾ ins long
Flight period: One, from April to June

Desert Swallowtail

The patterns on this type of butterfly vary a lot, but many desert butterflies have yellow bands or spots across black wings. They also have blue patches on the hindwings, and orange eyespots. Desert Swallowtails are fussy about where they live, so you will only spot them around desert washes and canyons. As no other swallowtails fly in these areas, this is a better identification tool than color or pattern. The caterpillars, ringed with green, cream, and black, like to feed on Queen Anne's lace and carrot plants. It is found in southern Nevada, southeastern Utah, southern California, western Arizona.

Species: *Papilio polyxenes rudkini*
Family: Papilionidae – About 2³/₄ ins long
Flight period: All year round, but most common in early spring

---

Rocky Mountain Skipper

Also known as the Draco Skipper. The male is dark brown with a big orange patch on its forewings, and also a large black mark. Females are bigger and mostly dark brown with a row of yellow marks on both wings. Underneath the wings, males and females are the same olive or greenish gray, and there are yellow spots on the hindwings. This butterfly lives in mountain meadows and lowlands, especially in the Rockies. It is found in the Rocky Mountain states and the Canadian Provinces.

Species: *Polites draco*
Family: Hesperiidae
About 1 ins long
Flight period: One, from June to August

Northern Blue

Males and females of this butterfly look completely different. Males have bright blue wings with a narrow dark border, but female wings are gray-brown with rows of orange spots around the margins. Underneath, the wings are dirty white, with a black line around the margins, orange spots inside this line, and scatterings of black spots on the rest of the wings. Look for the Northern Blue in mountains, heaths, bogs, and clearings. The caterpillars feed on lupines, crowberry, laurel, and Hudson Bay tea. It is found from Alaska to Maine, and south to Wisconsin.

Species: *Plebejus idas*
Family: Lycaenidae
1–1¹/₄ ins long
Flight period: One, from June to August

Keeping Records

You might like to keep a diary recording when and where you find your butterflies. Always take your field notebook with you when you go butterfly hunting. Make sketches of the area and the butterflies you see for your diary, or take photographs.

Butterfly diary

Keep your diary in a loose-leaf binder on separate sheets of paper. Fill out a sheet for each butterfly-hunting trip you go on with the details from your field notebook.

You can also write notes in it when you visit museums, or see a television program about butterflies. You can decorate it with your own drawings, photographs, pictures from magazines, postcards, and so on.

Butterfly walk

A good way to find out about butterflies in your neighborhood is by making a regular "butterfly walk." This is how to do it:

1 **Plan a route that takes about one hour to walk** (about 3 miles). Make sure it takes you past the different habitats in your neighborhood (like fields, woods, lakes, parks, etc.)

2 **Try to take this walk once a week** during the warmest time of the day and to do it in about one hour on each occasion. Try not to do it when the weather is wet or windy.

3 **Take your field notebook and this guidebook each time.**

4 **Record each butterfly you see** that comes within 15 ft of you, and how many there are.

Keeping a record

You can also record each species of butterfly that you see in a card index. The file should have a card for each species that gives detailed information like:

- the butterfly's common name, and its Latin name if known
- the family to which it belongs
- the date you saw it
- where you saw it: name and description of place
- the type of habitat
- the weather on the day of your visit
  You may be able to store your information on a computer. Keep an up-to-date printout, as well as your disk and its back-up.

5 **If you have to stop and identify a butterfly you don't recognize**, don't worry. Make a note of the time it takes you to identify the butterfly and add that time to the one hour your walk should take.

6 **Record your weekly information in a separate part of your butterfly diary.** Over the weeks, you will see which areas are best for butterflies and which species are most common at what time of year. Does your local pattern match the flight time information in this book?

Make a butterfly kite

Butterflies are so beautiful, they have inspired artists for centuries. Thousands of years ago, kite-makers in China made butterfly kites to flutter in the wind. You can make your own butterfly kite with some strong paper, two straws, some thin string, Scotch tape, and paints or markers.

1 **Draw an outline of a butterfly on a piece of paper.** Color in the wings with your paints or markers, giving them whatever pattern you like.

2 **When dry, cut the shape out from the paper,** being careful to keep it in one piece.

3 **Make some antennae from the string** and glue them to the butterfly's head.

4 **Place a long piece of string against the butterfly's body.** Lay the straws diagonally across the wings, on top of the string.

5 **Tape the straws down firmly** onto each of the four wing tips.

6 **Tie the string and the straws together** over the middle of the butterfly. Now your kite is ready to fly!

Woodlands & Clearings

The woodland habitat includes two quite different types of woods. Deciduous, broad-leaved forests are made up of trees that lose their leaves in winter, such as oak, beech, and ash. These trees have broad, flat leaves. Coniferous forests are green all year round, and include pines, firs, spruce, and redwoods. These trees have needle-like leaves.

Coniferous forests, which occur mostly in the West and North of North America, have few flowers growing on their floors because they let in so little sunshine. But some butterflies, such as the Pine White, like to feed on pine needles, so this lack of flowers does not matter.

Deciduous woodlands and forests are more common in the East. They let in plenty of light during the springtime to allow lots of wild flowers to grow on their floors. Here, you'll find butterflies drinking nectar, or resting on twigs and branches in sunny clearings (gaps among the trees). Don't forget to look for caterpillars munching on leaves and plants as well.

Clearings are found in both types of forest. They can be caused by the fall of a great tree that is at the end of its life, or by the actions of humans. The gap in the forest roof lets in sunlight and fast-growing plants take advantage of this before the slower-growing saplings shoot up to fill the hole. This picture shows eight species from this section; how many can you recognize?

Silvery Blue; Dun; Eastern Pine Elfin; Goatweed; Blue Mistletoe Hairstreak; Sleepy Orange; Silver Spotted Skipper; Pine White.

Woodlands & Clearings

Great Purple Hairstreak

This butterfly is also known as the Great Blue Hairstreak, and this suits its color much better. Males of this butterfly have brilliant, iridescent blue wings with a dark margin and green marks on the forewings. Females are a less bright blue. Both males and females have two tails on the end of their hindwings, one long and one short. Green caterpillars feed on mistletoe that grows on trees such as oaks, walnuts, and sycamores. Look for the Great Purple Hairstreak fluttering close to any trees that have mistletoe on them. It is found in the southeastern and southwestern U.S.

Species: *Atlides halesus*
Family: Lycaenidae
1¼–1½ ins long
Flight period: Two, from February to April, and from July to October

Blue Mistletoe Hairstreak

This butterfly is also called the Thicket Hairstreak, because it likes to fly around thickets and woodlands, sipping nectar from flowers. It has blue-gray wings, which are slightly brighter in the males. Underneath the wings are reddish brown with a black-edged white line which makes a "W" shape on the hindwing. The "Mistletoe" name comes from its caterpillars' favorite food, which they munch off pine, fir, and juniper trees. It is found from British Columbia to Mexico, east to Colorado.

Species: *Callophrys spinetorum*
Family: Lycaenidae
1–1¼ ins long
Flight period: One in the east, from June to July; two in the west, from March to September

Silvery Blue

The name of this butterfly applies to the male, which has silvery blue wings with dark margins. Females have dark brown wings, with a little blue on them. Underneath their wings, males and females are the same pale gray with black spots running across. The Silvery Blue does not fly very fast, and appears in early spring in woodlands, meadows, and canyons. Caterpillars' favorite plants include deer weed, lupine, wild pea, vetch, and locoweed. It is found east to west in Canada, and in the north of the U.S.

Species: *Glaucopsyche lygdamus*
Family: Lycaenidae
1–1¼ ins long
Flight period: One, from March to July

Western Tailed Blue

As its name suggests, this butterfly has a tail on each hindwing, although it is often not very noticeable. Males have lavender-blue wings with a narrow dark margin. Female wings are mostly brown with a little blue on them, and orange spots at the bottom of the hindwings. Underneath, males and females are white, with dark spots, and a faint orange mark on each hindwing. The Western Tailed Blue flies in moist meadows, waysides, on roadsides, and in clearings. Its caterpillars feed on locoweed, peas, and vetch. It is found from the West Coast states to Alaska.

Species: *Everes amyntula*
Family: Lycaenidae
1–1¼ ins long
Flight period: Two, from spring to fall

Bramble Green Hairstreak

Also known as the Coastal Green Hairstreak. This small butterfly's dark gray-brown wings have no pattern. Underneath, the wings are green, with some white dashes. It can be spotted flying around evergreen forests near the sea, wastelands, chaparral, and canyons, especially in the spring. Its caterpillars are bright green or red, and feed on deer weed, and California buckwheat. It is found on the mid-California coast, and southward.

Species: *Callophrys dumetorum*
Family: Lycaenidae
1–1¼ ins long
Flight period: One, from April to May

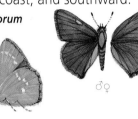

Brown Dusky Wing

Also known as Horace's Dusky Wing. Males of this butterfly are very dark brown, and females are lighter brown. Both males and females have patterns, mostly on their forewings. There are glassy white spots and brown fringes on the forewings also. It flies in clearings, along woodland edges, in waste areas, and any open grassy areas. Caterpillars feed on many different types of oaks. It is found in the eastern U.S. from the Mississippi River eastwards.

Species: *Erynnis horatius*
Family: Hesperiidae – 1¼–1¾ ins long
Flight period: Two to three, from January to October

Eastern Oak Dusky Wing

Also known as Juvenal's Dusky Wing, this butterfly's forewings are patterned with zigzag black and light brown marks, and tiny white marks near the tips. Hindwings are less patterned, with just a few mottled brown markings. A fringe runs all around the outside of the wings. As the name suggests, you'll find this butterfly in oak woodlands, basking in the sun with their wings spread out. Caterpillars feed on various types of oaks. It is found east of the Mississippi River and into southern Canada.

Species: *Erynnis juvenalis*
Family: Hesperiidae
1¼–1¾ ins long
Flight period: Two, from April to September

Banded Oak Dusky Wing

Also called the Sleepy Dusky Wing. With its gray forewings, and contrasting brown hindwings, this butterfly is two-tone. The forewings are well patterned with black wavy lines, and some white spots. Hindwings have some rows of light brown spots. Fringes all around the wings are brown. You may spot this butterfly in oak woodlands, or foothills. Its caterpillars feed on several different types of oaks and sometimes on American chestnut. It is found in the eastern U.S. northward, some in the Southeast.

Species: *Erynnis brizo*
Family: Hesperiidae
1¼–1¾ ins long
Flight period: One, from March to April

Northern Pearly Eye

This light-brown butterfly has dark eyespots that run in a straight line down its forewings. Each hindwing has five clear eyespots that curve around, following the shape of the wing. The Northern Pearly Eye does not mind shade, and you will find it in woodland clearings and waysides. It prefers feeding on tree sap than on flower nectar. The caterpillar is green with red-tipped horns, and feeds on grasses. It is found from Alberta to Nova Scotia, south to Louisiana.

Species: *Lethe anthedon*
Family: Satyridae – 1³/₄–2 ins long
Flight period: Two, from June to September

Dappled Marble

Can you see why this butterfly is also known as the Creamy Marblewing? The wings, with their creamy color and mottled markings, look a bit like marble. Underneath the hindwings is a green marbling effect. Look for the Dappled Marble flying low and fast around clearings, meadows, and lowlands. Its caterpillars are dark green and feed on buds, flowers, and some types of mustards. It is found from Alaska to Ontario to New Mexico and California.

Species: *Euchloe ausonia*
Family: Pieridae – 1¹/₂–1³/₄ ins long
Flight period: One to two, from February to August

Black Little Skipper

This name describes this small, black butterfly perfectly, but it is also known as the Roadside Skipper. Tiny white marks are at the top of each forewing, and the margins all around the edges of the wings are checkered. Underneath, the wings are brown and gray. This butterfly likes to fly around roadsides, as well as clearings, glades, and other grassy areas. Caterpillars feed on grasses. It is found west to east across northern U.S., but is absent from the Southwest.

Species: *Amblyscirtes vialis*
Family: Hesperiidae
³/₄–1 ins long
Flight period: One, from May to September

Sharp-veined White

Also called the Veined White, this butterfly is white with black spots and the clearly visible veins that give it its name. Underneath, the hindwings are creamy yellow, with clear dark scales. You can see the Sharp-veined White flying along waysides and in clearings and damp meadows. Its caterpillars are green with dark stripes. They feed on different kinds of mustard plants. It is found from Alaska to Newfoundland, West Coast of the U.S. and éast to New Mexico.

Species: *Pieris napi* – **Family:** Pieridae – 1¹/₂–1³/₄ ins long
Flight period: Two to three, from April to August

Hackberry Emperor

This butterfly gets its name from the hackberry trees that its caterpillars eat. It has a busy pattern of black, white, brown, and gray markings on its wings. Underneath, the wings are gray-blue. Look for this butterfly around hackberry trees in woodlands, or along trails. The Hackberry Emperor also ventures into suburbs and city streets. It is found from Minnesota to Arizona and Florida.

Species:
Asterocampa celtis
Family: Nymphalidae
1³/₄–2¹/₄ ins long
Flight period: Three, from March to October

Dogface Butterfly

Look closely at the forewing of this butterfly. Can you see a poodle's head at the edge of the black margin? The black spot looks like its eye. A yellow butterfly, the Dogface has an orangy color on its underside. Females do not have such a thick black margin on the edge of their wings. This butterfly lives around open woodlands, scrub, and desert. Its caterpillars are often green, and feed on clovers. It is found from southern California to Florida, migrates north to the Great Lakes.

Species: *Zerene cesonia*
Family: Pieridae
2–2¹/₂ ins long
Flight period: Continuous in the south; from June to August elsewhere

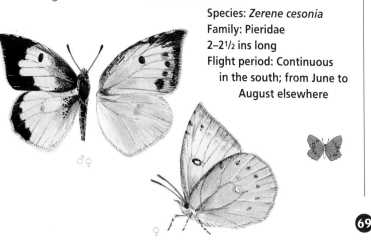

Pine White

The male of this butterfly has a white background with black tips, and gray veins on the hindwing. Females have a quite different yellow background, with orange margins on the hindwings. You will find the Pine White in pine and fir forests, fluttering high among the conifer trees. Sometimes they flutter down to take nectar from the forest floor. Their caterpillars are dark green with white stripes. They feed at the bottom of pines, true firs, and Douglas fir trees. It is found in British Columbia, the West Coast east to Dakota and south to New Mexico.

Species: *Neophasia menapia*
Family: Pieridae
1³/₄–2 ins long
Flight period: From July to September

Rambling Orange

Orange wings with thick black borders are the trademarks of this butterfly, which is sometimes called the Sleepy Orange. Underneath, the wings are pale yellow with brown blotches. Look for it flying rapidly in the summertime around fields, woodlands, and mountain canyons. Its caterpillars are thin and green with white, yellow, and black stripes. They munch on senna and clover. It is found in southern U.S. and Mexico, north to the Great Lakes.

Species: *Eurema nicippe*
Family: Pieridae
1¹/₂–2 ins long
Flight period: Continuous, from March to November in the north

Aphrodite Fritillary

An orange-brown color with black dashes and spots, females of this type of butterfly are larger than the males. Underneath, the hindwings have white spots. Look for crowds of these butterflies gathering to drink nectar from thistles, and many other flowers, around woodlands and wet meadows. They also like dry brushland, open woods, and prairies. Caterpillars, brown and spiny, feed on violets. It is found from East to West in the U.S. and Canada, as far as the Rockies.

Species: *Speyeria aphrodite*
Family: Nymphalidae – 1–2 ins long
Flight period: One, from June to September

Goatweed Butterfly

The male Goatweed Butterfly has bright orange wings, while the female is a duller orange, with brown marks. Underneath the wings, both males and females are purplish brown or gray, with brown marks. Look for the pointed tips on the forewings, and the tails on the hindwings. This butterfly lives around waysides, woodlands, and streams. Its caterpillars, which are greenish with warts and horns, feed on goatweeds, as the name suggests. It is found from Arizona to Kentucky and Florida.

Species: *Anaea andria*
Family: Nymphalidae
2¹/₂–3 ins long
Flight period:
From April to October

Harvester

Easy to spot with its orange color and brown borders and markings, the Harvester flies slowly around its damp woodland habitat. It visits twigs and leaves instead of flowers. If you look underneath the wings, you will see a pattern of dots and grayish circular markings. Caterpillars, which are greenish brown in color, are unusual because they are carnivores. Instead of plants, they eat wooly aphids, types of insects which live on trees and bushes. It is found in the eastern half of North America north to the Great Lakes.

Species: *Feniseca tarquinius*
Family: Lycaenidae
1¹/₄–1³/₄ ins long
**Flight period: Two in the north;
continuous in the south, from
February to December**

Comma Anglewing

A ragged outline and a sharp division between forewings and hindwings are the trademarks of this butterfly. Its wings are a reddish brown color with black blotches, with a row of yellow spots running down by the dark margin on each side. Underneath, you will see the reason for the name. There is a silver "comma" mark against a background of dark brown. Look for the Comma Anglewing darting about in clearings and waysides. You may also see it in woods and suburbs. Its caterpillars, light green and spiny, munch on hops and nettles. It is found from Saskatchewan to Texas, eastward.

♀

♂♀

Species: *Polygonia comma* – **Family:** Nymphalidae
1³/₄–2 ins long – **Flight period:** Three, from March to October

Question Mark

♂♀

This unusual name comes from a silver question mark shape with a white dot that is underneath the butterfly's hindwing. The Question Mark has ragged edges to its wings, which are bright rust-orange with black blotches. Its hindwings have long "tails." This butterfly's favorite food is sap and rotting fruit, which can sometimes make it a little drowsy if the fruit has fermented. It flies around woodlands, orchards, and streamsides. Caterpillars, which are rust-colored, feed on nettles, hops, elms, and hackberries. It is found from Saskatchewan to Arizona, eastward.

Species:
Polygonia interrogationis
Family: Nymphalidae
2¹/₂–2³/₄ ins long
Flight period: Continuous, from May to September

Comma Tortoise Shell

Also called the Compton Tortoise Shell. This butterfly has wide, ragged-edged wings which are orange with black and white marks at the top, and a rich rusty-brown color at the bottom. Underneath, the wings are gray-brown, with a silver comma or "V" shape on the hindwing. You may see this butterfly in clearings, or by waysides or streamsides, feeding on fallen fruit or sap. Caterpillars, pale green with black spines, feed on birches, willows, and poplars. It is found from British Columbia to Nova Scotia, and south to Colorado and Georgia.

♂♀

♂

Species: *Nymphalis vau-album*
Family: Nymphalidae
2¹/₂–3 ins long
Flight period: One, in July

Brown Dash

Also known as the Northern Broken Dash. A warm brown color with light markings, males of this butterfly have a dark dash on their forewings which is broken in two. Underneath, the wings are similar to above, except there is a pale crescent of yellow on the hindwings. The Brown Dash flies in wet woodlands, clearings, and fields. Its caterpillars feed on panic grass. It is found in the southeastern U.S., west to the Mississippi River.

Species: *Wallengrenia egeremet*
Family: Hesperiidae
1–1¼ ins long
Flight period: One, from May to September

Cobweb Little Skipper

Also known as the Lace-winged Roadside Skipper. A dark gray-brown above and below, this butterfly gets its name from the network of "cobwebs" underneath the hindwing. Forewings have a line of white marks running across them. This butterfly lives in wet woodlands. It is found in Connecticut south to Florida and west to Missouri and New Mexico.

Species: *Amblyscirtes aesculapius*
Family: Hesperiidae
1–1¼ ins long
Flight period: One in north, from January to September

Mottled Dusky Wing

This small butterfly's wings are mottled brown, as its name suggests. There are strong light and dark patches on the wings which almost look like bands. On the forewings, there are tiny white spots. You will find the Mottled Dusky Wing in woodland areas, and clearings. Its caterpillars, which are light green with white specks, feed on red rood in the east, and on buckbrush in Colorado. It is found east of the Mississippi River except Florida.

Species: *Erynnis martialis*
Family: Hesperiidae
1–1½ ins long
Flight period: Two, from May to July

Indigo Dusky Wing

Also called the Wild Indigo Dusky Wing. This butterfly's wings are dark brown and rounded. The forewings are patterned with light and dark markings and also with some glassy spots near the tips. A brown fringe runs along the outside of the wings. This butterfly's name comes from the plant that its caterpillars eat, and it can be seen along waysides and woodland edges, wherever wild indigo grows. It is found mostly east of the Mississippi River.

Species: *Erynnis baptisiae*
Family: Hesperiidae
1¼–1¾ ins long
Flight period: Several, from April to October

Dusted Skipper

This butterfly has pointed, dark brown wings. There are several white spots on the forewings, both above and underneath. Also underneath, there is a violet tinge of color toward the edge of the wings. You can see the Dusted Skipper in open fields, woodlands, and prairies, where it drinks nectar from blackberries, strawberries, and clover. Caterpillars feed on beard-grass. It is found from Saskatchewan to New England, south to New Mexico, Arkansas, and Georgia.

Species: *Atrytonopsis hianna*
Family: Hesperiidae
1¼–1½ ins long
Flight period: Two in the southeast, from March to April and in October; one in the north and west, from May to June

Western Skipper

Also known as the Woodland Skipper, because of its preferred habitat. Both males and females of this butterfly have orange and black forewings. Males have tawny hindwings; female hindwings are mostly brown. There are many different-looking versions of this butterfly, so it may be hard to identify. Look in woodlands, scrubland, roadsides, and waysides, where it may be sipping nectar from daisies. Its caterpillars munch grasses. It is found in British Columbia south to Baja California and east to Alberta, South Dakota, and Colorado.

Species: *Ochlodes sylvanoides*
Family: Hesperiidae
¾–1¼ ins long
Flight period: One, from June to October

Silver-spotted Skipper

The wings of this butterfly are rich brown, with orange marks on the forewing in the male, and similar pale yellow marks in the female. If you look underneath the hindwing, you will see the large silver spot that gives it its name. Fringes on the edges of the wings are checkered. The Silver-spotted Skipper can be seen in clearings, prairies, and canyons, but will venture into city parks and suburbs. Its caterpillars, which are light yellow-green, feed on wisteria, locusts, beggar's tick, beans, and licorice. It is found from West to East in the U.S., and some in the Southwest.

Species: *Epargyreus clarus*
Family: Hesperiidae – 1¾–2½ ins long
Flight period: One, from May to December

Cobweb Skipper

The wings of this butterfly are stubby and dark brown. There are orange marks on the male forewings, and white marks on those of the female. Underneath, the wings are olive-gray, with a web-like pattern of white veins, which gives the butterfly its name. Look for this skipper in fields, clearings, and grassy waysides. Caterpillars, brown with a greenish back stripe, feed on bluestem beard-grass. It is found in southern and eastern U.S., except coastal areas and Florida.

Species: *Hesperia metea*
Family: Hesperiidae
1–1½ ins long
Flight period: One, from March to April

Arizona Powdered Skipper

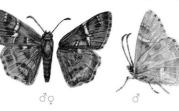

♂♀   ♂

An attractive pattern of light brown and tan marks covers the wings of this butterfly. There are white marks on the forewings, and the edge of the hindwings have wavy edges. Underneath, the wings look similar. This butterfly flies in open woody areas, desert canyons, and oases. It is found in the southwestern U.S. including Baja California and Mexico.

Species: *Systasea zampa*
Family: Hesperiidae – 1–1½ ins long
Flight period: Several, from April to October in Arizona

Southern Snout Butterfly

This big butterfly can be recognized by its dented forewing shape, by its color, which is brown, with white and orange marks, and by its big "snout" mouthparts. Underneath, the forewings are orange at the base, while the hindwings are pale sandy brown. The Southern Snout lives in canyons and woodland areas. It is found in all of the southern states of the U.S., northward to the Great Lakes.

Species: *Libytheana carinenta*
Family: Libytheidae
1¾–2 ins long
Flight period:
Continuous in the South

♂♀

Montane Skipper

Also called the Nevada Skipper. This butterfly has orange and brown wings. The forewings are orange at their base, and there are orange spots against a brown background on the hindwings. A brown margin runs around the wings. You can recognize males by the black mark on their forewings. Underneath the hindwing, you can see pale yellow marks. The Montane Skipper flies in clearings, grassy waysides, and high meadows. Caterpillars feed on western needlegrass in California, and on fescue in Colorado. It is found in British Columbia southward to Arizona.

Species: *Hesperia nevada*
Family: Hesperiidae
1–1½ ins long

Flight period: One, from May to July

♂♀

Dun Sedge Skipper

Also known as the Sedge Witch Skipper. You may not notice this butterfly easily, as it is pure brown, with no patterns. The only marks you can see on the wings are a black mark on the male forewing, and some tiny white spots on the female forewing. Underneath, the wings are a dull tan color. This butterfly flies in woodlands, fields, clearings, and waysides. It often lands on damp leaves. Caterpillars, which are shiny green, eat yellow nutgrass in Missouri, and sedge in Colorado. It is found in much of the U.S. and southern Canada.

Species: *Euphyes vestris*
Family: Hesperiidae
1–1¼ ins long
Flight period: Two,
from May to December

♂♀

♀

California Sister

This large butterfly has white bands running down its wings, with a bright orange blob at the tip of each forewing. The rest of the wings are brown. Underneath, the pattern is completely different, with pale blue, orange, cream, and brown bands and spots. This butterfly gets its name "sister" because its colors are like that of a nun's, or sister's habit. The California Sister flies in oak woods and foothills, and drinks from damp mud and fallen fruit. Caterpillars, dark green and brushlike, feed on types of oak. It is found from Washington State south to Mexico.

Species: *Adelpha bredowii*
Family: Nymphalidae – 3–3½ ins long
Flight period: Two, from April to October

Tawny Emperor

This butterfly is a tawny orange-brown color. All over its wings are darker bars and patches, including black and yellow spots. Females are much bigger than males, and a paler color. Underneath, the wings are pale, with brown areas. You may see this butterfly in woodlands near hackberry trees, or along waysides. The caterpillars are bright green and striped, and feed on hackberry trees. It is found from New Mexico to Maine and Florida.

Species: *Asterocampa clyton*
Family: Nymphalidae
2–2½ ins long
Flight period: Continuous in the South

White Admiral

You can recognize this butterfly by the wide black bands on its wings, and the bluish markings on the borders. There are also some red spots on the hindwings. The rest of the wings are brown or black. Look for White Admirals flapping and gliding, pursuing insects around woodlands and glades. Caterpillars, white, olive, and green, with bristles, feed on birches, willows, poplars, and hawthorns. It is found from Alaska to Florida, Arizona, and New Mexico.

Species: *Basilarchia arthemis*
Family: Nymphalidae
3–3¼ ins long
Flight period: Two, from June to August

Woodlands & Clearings

Western Pine Elfin

Male Western Pine Elfins have chocolate-brown wings with no pattern. Females are an orangy-brown color. Males and females have checkered margins all around the edges of their wings. Underneath, wings are patterned with zigzag marks in black, white, gray, and reddish-brown. Look out for this butterfly in spruce bogs, pine forests, and canyons. You may see it perching on shrubs, or sipping nectar from wild flowers. The caterpillars feed on the young shoots of pines, including lodgepole, and ponderosa pine. It is found in southwestern states, north and east to Maine.

Species: *Callophrys eryphon*
Family: Lycaenidae
3/4–1 ins long
Flight period: One, from May to June

Eastern Pine Elfin

Males of this butterfly have dark brown wings, and females' wings are lighter with orange blotches. Both males and females have their wings outlined with a black-and-white checkered edge. Underneath, the wings are strongly patterned with black zigzag marks, as well as white and brown colors. The Eastern Pine Elfin, as its name suggests, can be seen in pine and spruce woodlands. There, it sips nectar from wild plum, lupine, and other wild flowers. Its caterpillars, which are a transparent green color with white stripes, munch on the leaves of scrub pine, pitch, and jack pines. It is found in eastern U.S., except Florida, and Canada from the Great Lakes to Alberta.

Species: *Callophrys niphon*
Family: Lycaenidae
3/4–1¹/4 ins long
Flight period: One, from March to June

Woodland Elfin

Also called Henry's Elfin, this butterfly has very dark brown wings, especially in the male. Females may have an orangy-brown color on their wings. A good recognition mark to look for is the stumpy tail at the base of the hindwings. This butterfly lives in woodland edges, clearings, and scrubland, where it perches on twigs. Its caterpillars feed on flowers and also eat their way through fruits such as blueberries, wild plums, and Texas persimmons. It is found in the eastern half of the U.S.

Species: *Callophrys henrici*
Family: Lycaenidae – 1–1¹/4 ins long
Flight period: One, from March to April

Carolina Satyr

This dark brown butterfly may be a little confusing to identify, as it may or may not have eyespots on top of its wings. When present, the eyespots are small. Underneath, the wings have brown lines with a row of eyespots inside the margin. These eyespots have rims, and are blue on the inside. This butterfly likes moist areas, shade, and grasses, so you may see it in shady woodlands and in meadows, visiting flowers. Caterpillars, light green with dark green stripes, feed on different kinds of grasses. It is found in the southeastern U.S.

Species: *Hermeuptychia sosybius*
Family: Satyridae
1¹/4–1³/4 ins long
Flight period: Two, from March to October

Striped Hairstreak

On top, you can see no reason for this butterfly's name, as the wings are plain dark brown. But underneath, there are three broken stripes of black, bordered with white. There are also orange and blue marks near the tails. Look for the Striped Hairstreak high in the trees of woodlands, or within prickly hawthorn thickets. Caterpillars, green with yellow stripes, feed on oaks, willows, hollies, blueberries, plums, hawthorn, and rose bushes. It is found in three-fourths of the U.S., across southern Canada from British Columbia to Quebec.

Species: *Satyrium liparops*
Family: Lycaenidae
1–1½ ins long
Flight period: One, from July to August

Red-banded Hairstreak

Males of this butterfly have dark brown wings, but females look a little different, with blue patches on their wings. Underneath, the reason for the name is obvious. Across a background of light brown is a bright red band, edged with white and black. There is also a blue spot on each hindwing, near the two tails. The Red-banded Hairstreak flies along waysides and the margins of woodlands. Look for them just as it gets dark, as this is when they are most active. Their caterpillars are pale yellow and their favorite food includes dwarf sumac, cotton, and wax myrtle. It is only found in the Southeastern states.

Species: *Calycopis cecrops* – **Family:** Lycaenidae
¾–1 ins long – **Flight period:** Three, from April to October

Scrub Oak Hairstreak

Also called Edward's Hairstreak. Both above and underneath its wings, this butterfly is a warm brown color. There is a tiny tail on each hindwing. Although there is no pattern above, underneath the wings are streaks of dark brown spots ringed with white. There are also orange markings near the margin, as well as blue spots. The Scrub Oak likes to fly around scrub oak thickets. It has brownish caterpillars which feed on oaks, especially scrub oaks. It is found in the eastern U.S., but not throughout Southern states.

Species: *Satyrium edwardsii*
Family: Lycaenidae
1–1¼ ins long
Flight period: One, from June to July

Northern Metalmark

This butterfly's wings are chestnut brown on top and light orange underneath. There are black patterns both above and below. Shiny silvery marks run down the wings, giving it the name "metalmark." This butterfly prefers dry habitats such as forest clearings and meadows, especially where there is limestone. Green, hairy caterpillars with black spots feed on ragwort. It is found in Kentucky, Virginia, and Pennsylvania.

Species: *Calephelis borealis*
Family: Lycaenidae – 1–1¼ ins long
Flight period: One, from June to July

Find Out Some More

Useful Organizations

In addition to the national groups listed below, there are hundreds of local societies and groups studying butterflies and moths. Check with your teacher, or with your nearest natural history museum, wildlife refuge, or local public library for information on them.

The **Young Entomologist's Society** publishes a quarterly magazine containing general articles about insects which are of interest to the beginner. Write to: Young Entomologist's Society, 1915 Peggy Place, Lansing, Missouri 48910.

If you are also interested in moths, **The Lepidopterist's Society** publishes a journal and a newsletter. Write to: The Lepidopterist's Society, c/o Dr. William Winter, 257 Common Street, Dedham, Massachusetts 02026–4020.

The **Xerces Society** is another national society for butterfly enthusiasts. Write to: Xerces Society, c/o Melody Allen, 10 Southwest Ash Street, Portland, Oregon 97204.

On the West Coast, write to: **Butterfly Lovers International**, c/o Dr. Stevanne Auerbach, 210 Columbus Avenue No. 611, San Francisco, California 94133

Also on the West Coast, The **Lepidoptera Research Foundation** is for professional entomologists and serious amateurs. Write to: Lepidoptera Research Foundation, 9620 Heather Road, Beverley Hills, California 90210.

Many of the preserves owned by the **Nature Conservancy** and its chapters conserve unique and threatened habitats for insects. Write to: Nature Conservancy, Suite 800, 1800 North Kent Street, Arlington, Virginia 22209.

In Canada, the **Canadian Nature Foundation** is a good starting point. Write to: Canadian Nature Foundation, 453 Sussex Drive, Ottawa, Ontario K1N 6Z4.

Places To Visit

Butterflies are part of the vast insect order—they can be found virtually everywhere, from wild prairies to city sidewalks. Here is a selection of different habitats where butterflies can be found:

Cape May, New Jersey: Jutting far out into Delaware Bay, this is a major gathering point for migrating Monarchs from late August to early October, as well as large numbers of Painted Ladies, Buckeyes, Sulfurs, and other species.

Florida Keys: Tropical butterflies can be found in the few remaining, undisturbed islands of the Keys. Good places to visit are **Key Deer** National Wildlife Refuge and **Biscayne** National Park.

Santa Ana National Wildlife Refuge, Alamo, Texas: This and several neighboring refuges (including **Laguna Atascosa** National Wildlife Refuge,) preserve subtropical forest where butterflies abound. More than 300 species have been recorded here—the greatest number anywhere in the U.S.

Rocky Mountain National Park, Estes Park, Colorado: Rising to 12,000 feet in places, this park has a variety of habitats including high meadows where tundra species like arctics and alpines can be found.

Natural Bridges State Park, Santa Cruz, California: The largest of several wintering sites for Monarchs in southern California.

Commercial "butterfly gardens," exhibiting native and exotic species, include: **Butterfly World**, Coconut Creek, Florida; **Day Butterfly Center**, Callaway Gardens, Pine Mountain, Georgia; and **Butterfly World**, Marine World Africa U.S.A., Vallejo, California.

There are also many preserves and refuges in every state—check with your teacher, or with your nearest natural history museum, wildlife refuge, or local public library for information on them.

Index & Glossary

To find the name of an insect in this index, search under its main name. So, to look up Brown Elfin; look under Elfin, not under Brown. The names of butterfly families are shown in **Bold** type.

A

abdomen the third section of an insect's body. It carries the *ovipositor* 6

Admiral,
 Red, 15
 White, 75

Alfalfa butterfly, 16

Alpine,
 Common, 36
 Red-disk, 22
 Spruce-bog, 22
 White-spot, 22

alpine meadow a high meadow found on mountains above the timberline 29

Anglewing,
 Comma, 71
 Faunus, 29

Apollo,
 American, 27
 Small, 10

Arctic,
 Banded, 47
 Brown, 36
 Forest, 22
 Mottled, 47

Azure, Spring, 15

B

Baltimore, 24

Blue,
 Acmon, 10
 Common, 34
 Greenish Clover, 24
 High Mountain, 44
 Lupine, 34
 Northern, 61
 Orange-margined, 34
 Primrose, 44
 Silver-studded, 10
 Silvery, 66
 Tailed, 10
 Western Tailed, 66

Brown, 22, 23, 36, 37, 44, 46, 47, 68, 76

Brown, Marsh-eyed, 23

Buckeye, 37

C

Cabbage butterfly, 10

camouflage having the appearance or the coloring of a habitat or plant, so that the butterfly or *caterpillar* is not easily seen 11

caterpillar a young stage of the butterfly when it looks very different to the adult 4

Checkerspot,
 Gorgone, 48
 Great Plains, 48
 Silvery, 37
 Streamside, 37

Cloudy Wing,
 Eastern, 38

 Northern, 44
 Southern, 38

Comma, Green, 29

Copper,
 American, 48
 Bronze, 16
 Cinquefoil, 26
 Cranberry Bog, 26
 Flame, 48
 Forest, 26
 Gray, 44
 Great Gray, 44
 Mariposa, 26
 Purplish, 35
 Small, 48

Crescent, Pale, 60

Crescentspot,
 Field, 49
 Pallid, 60
 Pearl, 49
 Pearly, 49

D

Dash,
 Brown, 72
 Long, 38
 Northern Broken, 72

dimorphic means the male and female don't look anything like each other, 39, 51

Dogface butterfly, 69

Dusky Wing,
 Aspen, 23
 Banded Oak, 67
 Brown, 67
 Columbine, 56
 Dreamy, 23
 Eastern Oak, 67
 Hairy, 47
 Horace's, 67

Useful Books

Amazing Butterflies and Moths, John Still (EYEWITNESS JUNIORS, Alfred A. Knopf).

Butterflies: How to Identify and Attract Them to Your Garden, Marcus Schneck (Rodale Press).

Golden Guide to Moths and Butterflies, Robert T. Mitchell & Herbert S. Zim (Golden Press).

Handbook for Butterfly Watchers, Robert M. Pyle (Houghton Mifflin Co.).

Insect & Spider Collections of the World, R.H. Arnett & A. Samuelson (Flora & Fauna Publications, Gainesville, Florida), Find out where your nearest collection of butterflies is housed.

Peterson First Guide: Caterpillars, Amy Bartlett Wright (Houghton Mifflin Co.).

Peterson Field Guides: Eastern Butterflies, Opler & Malikui (Houghton Mifflin Co.).

Peterson Field Guides: Western Butterflies, Tilden & Smith (Houghton Mifflin Co.).

Index & Glossary

Indigo, 72
Juvenal's, 67
Mottled, 72
Persius, 47
Sleepy, 67
Wild Indigo, 72

E
Elfin,
 Brown, 14
 Eastern Pine, 76
 Henry's, 76
 Hoary, 24
 Western Pine, 76
 Woodland, 76
Emperor,
 Hackberry, 69
 Tawny, 75

F
Fire-rim, 37
Fritillary,
 Aphrodite, 70
 Atlantis, 28
 Bog, 29
 Freya's, 26
 Great Spangled, 49
 Meadow, 48
 Ocellate, 29
 Purple Bog, 29
 Regal, 28
 Silver Meadow, 49
 Silver-bordered, 49
 Titania's, 29
 Variegated, 48
 Willow-bog, 26
 Zigzag, 26

G
Giant Skipper,
 Plains Yucca, 41

Strecker's, 41
Glassy Wing, Little, 38
Goatweed butterfly, 70

H
habitat a particular type of landscape, 10
Hairstreak,
 Acadian, 25
 Banded, 14
 Behr's, 58
 Blue Mistletoe, 66
 Bramble Green, 67
 Coastal Green, 67
 Common, 14
 Coral, 45
 Edward's, 77
 Gray, 14
 Great Blue, 66
 Great Purple, 66
 Northern Willow, 25
 Orange, 58
 Red-banded, 77
 Scrub Oak, 77
 Striped, 77
 Sylvan, 56
 Thicket, 66
 Western Willow, 56
 White-M, 34
Harvester, 70
Hesperidae, 12, 13, 16, 23, 24, 27, 34, 35, 38, 39, 40, 41, 44, 46, 47, 51, 56, 57, 59, 61, 67, 68, 72, 73, 74
Hoary Edge, 38

L
legumes plants belonging to the pea and bean

family, 44
Lycaenidae, 10, 14, 15, 16, 24, 25, 26, 34, 35, 44, 45, 48, 56, 58, 61, 66, 67, 70, 76, 77

M
Marble,
 Dappled, 68
 Rosy, 45
Marblewing,
 Creamy, 68
 Olympian, 45
Metalmark,
 Gray, 56
 Mesquite, 56
 Mormon, 14
 Northern, 77
 Swamp, 25
Milkweed, 17
Monarch, 17
Mourning Cloak, 11

N
Nymph, Large Wood, 37
Nymphalidae, 11, 15, 24, 26, 28, 29, 37, 48, 49, 60, 69, 70, 71, 75

O
Orange,
 Rambling, 69
 Sleepy, 69
Orange Tip, Sara, 45
 Western, 45
ovipositor the egg-laying device on the *abdomen* of the adult female insect 39

P
Painted Lady, 15
 American, 29
Parnassian, Clodius, 27
 Small, 10
Pearly Eye, Northern, 68
 Southern, 23
predator a hunter, usually carniverous (a meat eater), 11
proboscis the tubular, sucking mouthpieces of some insects, 6

Q
Question Mark, 71

R
Rambler, Roadside, 13
Ringlet, 46

S
Sachem, 46
Satyr,
 Carolina, 76
 Grasshopper, 44
 Little Wood, 36
sedges a group of plants with rows of narrow, pointed leaves found in marshy land, 24
Silver Spike, Morrison's, 59
Sister, California, 75
Skipper,
 Alpine Checkered, 35
 Arizona Powdered, 74
 Arrowhead, 59
 Beard-grass, 47
 Black Little, 68
 Black-dust, 51

Black-vein, 46
Blazing Star, 40
Broad Marsh, 27
Broad Winged, 27
Brown-rim, 47
Checkered, 13
Clouded, 35
Cobweb, 73
Cobweb, Little, 72
Common Branded, 39
Crossline, 59
Delaware, 46
Draco, 61
Dun Sedge, 74
Dusted, 73
Eastern Sedge, 40
Fiery, 51
Golden-banded, 40
Gray, 13
Green, 51
Greenish Little, 12
Hobomok, 39
Holarctic Grass, 39
Indian, 41
Lace-winged
Roadside, 72
Leonardus, 40
Long-tailed, 34
Montane, 74
Nevada, 74
Northern Dimorphic,
 39
Northern Grizzled, 35
Ottoe, 39

Pahaska, 59
Palmetto, 40
Pepper & Salt, 12
Prairie, 39
Roadside, 68
Rocky Mountain, 61
Saltgrass, 12
Sandhill, 12
Sedge Witch, 74
Silver-spotted, 73
Southern Dimorphic,
 51
Swarthy, 39
Tawny-edged, 12
Two-spot Sedge, 24
Uncas, 57
Western, 73
White-veined, 57
Woodland, 73
Yellow-dust, 59
Yellow-patch, 40
Yucca Giant, 57
Zabulon, 51
Skipperling,
 Arctic, 41
 Black-veined, 59
 European, 46
 Garita, 23
 Least, 41
 Sunrise, 59
 Western, 23
Snout, 74
Snout butterfly,
 Southern, 74

Sooty Wing,
 Common, 13
 Goldenheaded, 56
 Redhead, 56
Sulfur,
 Cloudless, 16
 Common, 50
 Dainty, 58
 Golden, 27
 Little, 50
 Orange, 16
 Pink-edged, 50
 Queen Alexandra's, 51
 Ultraviolet, 51
 Western, 27
 Wolf-face, 45
Swallowtail, 10, 11,
 12, 13, 17, 25, 27,
 36, 57, 58, 61
Swallowtail,
 American, 13
 Anise, 11
 Black, 13
 Cliff, 57
 Desert, 61
 Giant, 12
 Pale Tiger, 25
 Pipevine, 11
 Short-tailed Black, 57
 Spicebush, 17
 Tiger, 17
 Western, 11
 Western Tiger, 58
 Zebra, 36

T

thorax the middle section of an insect's body. It is divided into three segments, each of which carries a pair of legs. The back two carry the wings if they exist, 6

Tortoiseshell,
 Comma, 71
 Compton, 71
 Milbert's, 37

V

Viceroy, 28

W

Whirlabout, 16
White, 10, 16, 27, 45,
 50, 51, 58, 60, 68, 69
White,
 Checkered, 60
 Pine, 69
 Sharp-veined, 68
 Small, 10
 Spring, 60
 Veined, 68
 Western, 60
Yellow,
 Dwarf, 58
 Little, 50
 Mexican, 45